Get Promoted

Brandon Tolbert

DEDICATION

I dedicate this book to all those with real intent on progressing their lives and reaching their full potential. I write with those individuals and teams in mind who wish to "promote" their lives by learning the techniques and leadership skills to better serve others and increase their influence in their personal and professional life. A special dedication to all those men and women serving or who have served in our armed forces. Without your sacrifice, none of us would have the freedom to reach our potential and **PROMOTE** our lives.

"We know what we are but know not what we may be."
William Shakespeare

CONTENTS

ACKNOWLEDGMENTS

First and foremost, I would like to express my deepest gratitude to my wonderful wife and biggest supporter, Marianne. She has endured many late nights as my sounding board and initial editor! Next, I must thank my three amazing children who are the inspiration in my life to continue stepping outside my comfort zone to reach new levels of achievement and promotion.

In addition, no accomplishment in my life has come without great mentors and heroes I will always appreciate and admire for leading by example and charting a course for me to follow. Here are a few I feel must be mentioned by name to show my sincere appreciation for their impact in my life:

Dan Tolbert – My father and best friend. The perfect example.

Elaine Tolbert – My mother and nurturer. The glue to our family.

My four older brothers – Toby, Alan, Curt, and David. You taught me life's most important lessons from the very beginning, and you let me win! I'm still learning from your examples and still winning because of you!

My mentors and closest friends. Too many to name them all but these few must get in print for having such a positive long term impact on my personal and professional life. Roy Sanford, Craig Cluff, Lonnie Schrader, Troy Parker, John Collins, Warren Lenfant, Randy King, Doug Nash, John Casey, Rick Dalberg, David Lacko, Jeff Thornton, Cesar Valenzuela, David Leech, and Gerald Topley.

I thank you all and countless others from the bottom of my heart! Without the support, dedication, and sacrifice of all these exceptional people, this book would have never been brought to life. In addition, all those who choose to follow these proven leadership techniques and life principles in order to GET PROMOTED would have never had this opportunity.

Thank You!

INTRODUCTION

Promotion: The act of furthering the growth or development of something. In this case, **YOU!**

What if as a result of completing this book you could improve every aspect of your life? What if you could use the techniques described to promote your relationships with your spouse, children, friends, and associates? What if you could promote your career, business, or financial status beyond levels of success ever before seen? What if you could use the same techniques to increase your level of influence in every interaction or team you lead?

Isn't promoting one's life the central purpose across every culture, society, and religion? Maybe it's because within each of us lies a core need for eternal progression. It's a simple need to reach our potential.

There once was a nurse who was assigned to take care of the critically ill patients in a particular hospital. She began asking her patients this simple question, "Any regrets or things you would do differently with your life?" What she discovered was a very common theme and particularly these three common responses:

1. I wish I had spent more time with the ones I love.

2. I wish I had allowed myself to be happy.

3. I wish I had done more to reach my full potential.

Taking the time to study this book, learning from the examples, and implementing the lessons and techniques in your life will assist you in conquering these three regrets!

Several years ago I read a book from one of my favorite coaches and life mentors Bobby Bowden. The book is titled The Bowden Way. Bobby signed it for me and I keep a copy on my desk to this day. Bobby began that book expressing his commitment to being "old fashioned".

I will begin this work in similar fashion. Although I am not quite as old in years as Coach Bowden, I am very "old fashioned" as he explained. Not in the way many describe but in a different way.

Let me explain what I mean by *old-fashioned*. Many truths persist through time. Certain ways of doing things continue to work decade after decade, and century after century. As we learn from experience and many great leaders who came before us, the recipe for leadership and personal growth (promotion) existed long before we took the stage and will stand true long after we are gone.

This is the "old fashion" I'm also committed to! Only fools dismiss previous successes when dealing with leadership. Leadership is an art and self-development and promoting is included in the arts, not science. The techniques described in this book are simply recipes used by the great leaders for generations that I have simply emulated in my life to resolve similar outcomes and levels of success.

Are great recipes tinkered with from time to time? Of course! Our life experience and ever-changing environment requires certain "tinkering" as we lead and promote. However, the core principles will never change because leadership is about PEOPLE. People come to this life with certain needs and emotions that can only be managed through proper application of the art of leadership. For every reader to get the most out of this work, they must turn inward. YOU must look to yourself for change in order to begin the process of PROMOTING your life!

The act of looking inward is difficult. In fact, your success at promoting your life hinges nearly 100% on your ability to understand this single point. As I said, it's an art not science, so **NO ONE** can give you a pill or formula that will change the way you think. This one thing that will determine the outcome **MUST COME FROM WITHIN**.

When things go well it becomes easy to look inward, right? When things are not going as planned it becomes much more difficult. I will share a personal experience that relates in a small and simple way. My son and I were throwing a football back and forth in our house one afternoon. At the time he was just 3 years old so I was literally sitting in a chair while he was standing a few feet away. We were in the process of selling our home at the time and had potential buyers on their way to walk through the house with our agent. My wife had just cleaned the area we were playing in and instructed us to, "Stop playing in the house before you break something!" Unfortunately, that direction was ignored from two knuckleheads having a good time. Another step at preparing the home for the walk through was lighting some scented candles. I think you see where I'm going with this story, but allow me to finish. I got temporarily distracted and looked away from my son just long enough for him to throw the football without my seeing it. I felt the ball whip by my head and heard a loud crash! I looked up at him, not wanting to look behind me where the crash came from. His eyes were wide open and he pointed at the wall behind me. I turned to see the disaster. One entire wall and two windows were now covered in hot wax which was the color red! The broken porcelain candle holder on the floor in pieces and hot wax everywhere.

I turned to him and said, "Dude, why did you throw it?" and he replied, "Why didn't you catch it"! Clearly, we both immediately looked **OUTWARD** to place blame and avoid the wrath we heard bouncing down the stairs in the form of mom! Just moments earlier, I would brag about a great catch when I made one and he would brag about a great throw. When times are "good" we love to look **INWARD**, yet when times get tough we tend to do the opposite.

Many describe this behavior as "human nature". I disagree! I believe it's a learned behavior. I believe we are taught from many life experiences to react in this way. This is the good news because learned behavior is much easier to alter and redirect with determination and commitment. I challenge every reader to begin your personal promotion process this day by **changing the way you think** and alter your learned behavior by looking inward first for promoting your life. It is imperative you learn to challenge your thoughts before they become your actions.

CHANGING YOUR MIND

Years ago there were two young boys who were cousins, rarely seen apart. They spent countless hours together playing, working, camping, riding ATV's, and much more. The older of the two (James) being three years older, taller, stronger, and more mature in stature pretty much led the way. The younger boy (Billy) admired his older cousin and allowed James to take charge. James grew more and more confident in his role as the leader and would even take advantage of his role as many often do. James enjoyed playing sports with Billy where he could use his size and maturity to dominate and win, keeping Billy in his "place".

One day it all changed. James' parents had recently bought him boxing gloves and it was time to put them to the test. James seeing Billy as an easy target said, "Hey Billy, lets fight with my new gloves like real boxers!" Billy being a little concerned but not wanting to disappoint his older cousin agreed.

James began punching Billy in the face and using his significant reach advantage to keep Billy's attempts to counter-punch at bay. The punches came with more pop and the intensity was rising with every blow to Billy's head. Billy, now doing his best to hold back the tears, partially from pain but mostly from the heart break of the situation; stepped back far enough to get out of James' reach for a quick recovery. Billy looked down as to not allow James to see the tears. Staring at his hands in his boxing gloves by his side, Billy made a decision that shaped many more to come throughout his life.

He "changed his mind". He decided he would no longer give James the power and respect, but would BELIEVE in himself.

Billy had grown up being the youngest of five boys who were very active and constantly battling each other through sports and competition. Billy knew "physically" he was tough and the pain from James' punches was really not bad compared to so many other things in Billy's life, physically. Billy had GIVEN James the power "mentally" to win.

In a few split seconds staring down at his gloves that day, Billy "changed his mind" and decided it was time to also change the direction of this fight. Billy clutched those gloves and resolved to get close enough to James to unleash his wrath and land some punches of his own. Billy looked up at James with a determination to win this fight. James immediately noticed a different "look" from Billy. Billy charged James and broke past the reach advantage to get close enough to reach his goal. Billy landed about ten consecutive punches on James, knocking him to the ground. Covering up for protection James cried, "I quit!"

That day Billy became SUCCESS CONSIOUS. Billy went on to accomplish many things in his life that others said were impossible. He continues to this day all because he understands the art of "changing your mind".

As Napoleon Hill describes in his best seller Think and Grow Rich, there is an art to "changing your mind" from *FAILURE CONSCIOUS* to *SUCCESS CONSCIOUS*. Success comes to those who become SUCCESS CONSCIOUS. Failure comes to those who indifferently allow themselves to become FAILURE CONSCIOUS, period.

I believe we are all oak trees within the acorn. We are all seedlings of success within our mind. The most powerful and beautiful aspect, NO ONE but YOU can control your mind or thoughts which lead to your success!

Billy didn't alter the outcome of that boxing match and other events in his life by making excuses or accepting the "perceived" expected outcome. He made a conscious decision to change the direction of the event and subsequent events to follow by looking INWARD for the answer, never looking outward for an excuse. How easy could it have been for Billy to excuse losing the boxing match to a bigger, stronger, and older cousin?

How many times in our lives do we accept failure because it's "excusable".

Wherever you find a problem, you will usually find excuses and the finger-pointing of blame. Society has become addicted to playing the victim and "passing the buck".

Stephen Covey made this point clear in his book _The Seven Habits of Highly Effective People_. _"If only my boss wasn't such a controlling idiot…If only I hadn't been born so poor….If only I lived in a better place….If only I hadn't inherited such a temper from my dad….If only my kids weren't so rebellious….If only the other department didn't mess up orders all the time….If only we weren't in such a declining industry….If only our people weren't so lazy and without drive….If only my wife was more understanding….**If only….If only.**"_

Blaming everyone and everything else for our problems and challenges may be the norm and may provide temporary relief from the pain, but it also chains us to these very problems. Show me someone who is humble enough to accept and take responsibility for his or her circumstances and courageous enough to take whatever initiative necessary to creatively work his or her way through or around these challenges, and I'll show you the supreme power of choice.

The survival response of popular culture is cynicism...."just lower your expectations of life to the point that you aren't disappointed by anyone or anything." The contrasting principle of growth and hope throughout history is the discovery that "**I am the creative force of my life**."

This thought process is critical to understand before you proceed another minute on this journey to create balance and promote your standard of living. We will touch on this throughout the following chapters as a reminder, but take a moment now to self-assess where you generally fall on the pendulum. Do you look "inward" for responsibility and control or do you look "outward" to blame or excuse the outcome to some exterior force?

Henry Ford is well known for his successes and achievements. One story surrounding the creation of his now famous V-8 motor illustrates the real key to his success. When Ford decided to produce this motor with eight cylinders cast in one block, he instructed his engineers to design and produce the engine. The design was placed on paper but the engineers had bad news for Mr. Ford. To create a V-8 motor from a single block was simply IMPOSSIBLE!

Ford replied, "Produce it anyway." "But", they replied, "It's impossible!" "Go ahead," Ford directed, "And stay on the job until you succeed no matter how much time is required".

So the engineers did as directed. Six months went by, nothing happened. Another six months, still nothing. The engineers tried every conceivable plan to carry out the orders, but the task seemed out of the question; "impossible!"

At the end of the year Ford checked on the progress. Again, he was informed it was impossible. He replied, "Go right ahead, I want it and I will have it." They went ahead and as we all know, the secret was found and the V-8 motor was produced!

DETERMINATION was the key to Ford's success.

"Our brains become magnetized with the dominating thoughts which we hold in our minds, and, by means with which no man is familiar, these "magnets" attract to us the forces, the people, and the circumstances of life which harmonize with the nature of our dominating thoughts."
Napoleon Hill

How powerful can our thoughts become? A long time ago there was a great warrior who faced a situation which made it necessary for him to make a decision which insured his success on the battlefield. He was about to send his armies against a powerful foe, whose men outnumbered his own. He loaded his soldiers into boats, sailed to the enemy's country, unloaded all soldiers and equipment, then gave the order to burn the ships that carried them there. Addressing his men before the first battle, he said, "You see the boats going up in smoke? That means that we cannot leave these shores alive unless we win! We now have no choice....we win or we perish!" They won.

As positive and elevating the trained mind can be, it can also be trained to bind and limit your potential. I read a story once that illustrates the binding power of the trained mind.

A man vacationing in Africa was stunned to encounter a herd of elephants walking down a road in an orderly procession being led by a trainer. The animals were attached by a thin chain linked around their front legs. "I don't understand," the man said to the trainer. "How can these powerful beasts be contained by such a weak line?"

"We use a similar chain to restrict their movements when they are young," the trainer replied. "They are 'taught' to believe that the chain will restrict them even though they are bigger, stronger, and could easily break free."

The man was left speechless. The elephants were imprisoned by cruelty and conditioning from knowing their own power!

The same is true for each of us. How often do we "condition" ourselves or loved ones in a similar manner? Negativity, fear, discouragement, lack of confidence, and support are just a few tactics we employ to "train" ourselves and others to embrace less than what we are capable. The change must come from within to "break our chains" and release our true potential.

Over the years, I have had the opportunity to travel and lead many teams. Every single time I approach a new team and begin the process of "changing their mind" about their performance and future, I am met with statements and beliefs such as "we can't do that here" or "that's never been done here". It has become comical at this point in my life and career, but without fail, when you challenge others to reach new uncharted results or potential, you will expose their "chains". What "chains" are tied to your progression?

I often witness aspiring leaders get inspired and committed to change. They begin training themselves to act differently, build their self-confidence, and begin to separate themselves by going the "extra mile". Unfortunately, many find themselves in a lonely place and quickly revert back to a life of mediocrity and acceptance among the sheep!

Breaking our chains will never come easy and will never be popular among those who see your success as their failure. Commit to a life of never ending progress and discard those who place limits or "chains" on your vision. In most cases WE are the one's placing limits on our vision and capacity.

You will find success when you first RESOLVE mentally to do whatever it takes, no matter the challenges, no matter the critics, no matter the current circumstance, no matter the pain, and PERSIST toward your vision until it becomes reality.

To more clearly understand the POWER of the mind you must understand the law behind the SELF-CONFIDENCE FORMULA.

SELF-CONFIDENCE FORMULA as described by Napoleon Hill:

First. *I know that I have the ability to achieve the object of my definite purpose in life, therefore, I DEMAND of myself persistent, continuous action toward its attainment, and I here and now promise to render such action.*

Second. *I realize the dominating thoughts of my mind will eventually reproduce themselves in outward, physical action, and gradually transform themselves into physical reality,* *therefore, I will concentrate my thoughts for thirty minutes daily, upon the task of thinking of the person I intend to become, thereby creating in my mind a clear mental picture of that person.*

Third. *I know through the principle of auto-suggestion, any desire that I persistently hold in my mind will eventually seek expression through some practical means of attaining the object back of it, therefore, I will devote ten minutes daily to demanding of myself the development of SELF-CONFIDENCE.*

Fourth. *I have clearly written down a description of my DEFINITE CHIEF AIM in life, and I will never stop trying, until I shall have developed sufficient self-confidence for its attainment.*

Fifth. *I fully realize that no wealth or position can long endure, unless built upon truth and justice, therefore, I will engage in no transaction which does not benefit all whom it affects. I will succeed by attracting to myself the forces I wish to use, and the cooperation of other people. I will induce others to serve me, because of my willingness to serve others. I will eliminate hatred, envy, jealousy, selfishness, and cynicism, by developing love for all humanity, because I know that a negative attitude toward others can never bring me success. I will cause others to believe in me, because I will believe in them, and in myself.*

Supporting this formula is a law of Nature which no man has been able to explain. The psychologists have named this law "auto-suggestion". The most important aspect we have to learn of this law is that IT WORKS! All impulses of thought have a tendency to clothe themselves in their physical equivalent.

Just as electricity will turn the wheels of industry, and render useful service if used constructively; or snuff out life if wrongly used, so will the law of "auto-suggestion" lead you to peace and prosperity or down into the valley of misery, failure, and death, all according to your degree of understanding and application of it. Use it wisely!

Clearly, the first step to reaching your potential is somewhere in your brain cells. It lies there sleeping, the seed of achievement which, if aroused and put into action, would carry you to heights you have never known.

There is a major difference between WISHING for a thing and being READY to receive it. No one is ready to receive it until he BELIEVES he can accomplish it. Until our state of mind is one of BELIEF in self, not mere hope or wish, we will never reach our full potential. Begin the process of "changing your mind" and you will find immediate results and successes in every area of your life.

"Change your thoughts and you change your world."
Norman Vincent Peal

PYGMALION EFFECT

Ever heard of the Pygmalion Effect? I guarantee you have in one way or another without knowing it. In fact, if you've ever had a great leader in your life or have ever been a great leader or mentor for others, you've seen the "Pygmalion Effect" in action!

So what is it exactly and why do I want to talk about it now? The Pygmalion Effect is the phenomenon in which the greater the expectation placed upon people, the better they will perform. The work of Robert Rosenthal and Lenore Jacobson (1968), among others, shows that teacher expectations influence student performance. Positive expectations influence performance positively, and negative expectations influence performance negatively. This phenomenon has been proven over and over again in scientific studies yet so few people take advantage of it.

When I mentor and coach any leader from parents to trainers, managers, coaches, etc. I always start with a clear understanding of this key principle. First, how do they currently interact with their subordinates vs *The Pygmalion Effect*? This proves to be a great starting point in growing their leadership skills and improving performance.

The research that has been conducted since Rosenthal's and Jacobson's original study has determined that *The Pygmalion Effect* applies to all kinds of settings from sports teams, to military, to the corporate workplace. Therefore, the great news from all this research and study is that you can elevate the achievement of others if you practice a few simple steps. There is no magic pill to take, just an attitude of having higher expectations for those who you have influence which will lead to better results! I mentioned earlier the many teams I have had the privilege of leading throughout the years and how every single one of them had "chains" to break. Amazingly, every single one of those teams also BROKE THE CHAINS and found new levels of achievement simply by creating a foundation built on this concept.

What I would like to do is take The Pygmalion Effect and apply it to YOU! We are focusing this book, guide, or educational course on getting ourselves "promoted", right? How do we apply this phenomenon to ourselves? You must begin to treat yourself and hold yourself accountable to acting the way you wish to become.

Here are a few simple things you can do to start making this work for you.

1.   Raise Expectations of Yourself

We often find the "superstar" employees carry a heavy load of the work and for good reason. The more we expect from them and more we assign them, the more they seem to accomplish and find a way to "rise to the occasion". We use statements like..."*I wouldn't be giving you this, but I know you can handle it.*" Once again proving our attitude of expecting promising results as we assign additional workload or projects. They are actually thinking......"*well, if my (parent, boss, coach, or teacher) thinks I can do it, I guess I can!*"

We treat the superstars differently because we don't have mental limits on them. We find ourselves more open to their suggestions, comments, or concerns. We give them praise openly and our confidence grows each day as we gain trust. We tend to have less stress around them because of the elevated trust and confidence. **All of which we must learn to apply to our most important "superstar".....ourselves!**

The German writer/philosopher Johann Wolfgang Von Goethe once said....***"If you treat an individual as he is, he will remain how he is. But if you treat him as if he were what he ought to be and could be, he will become what he ought to be and could be."***

Start today by imagining who you want to become and start treating yourself as if you already are. You must become the leader before you will gain the title.

2.   Silent Committing Yourself

Silent committing is one of the most under-utilized tools in the communication tool box. Mostly because many simply do not understand the art of communication and this simple technique that will solidify and greatly improve the chances of success in accomplishing a task, mission, or goal.

Silent committing is simply bringing outside influence into the equation. For example, if I were to commit you to losing 10 lbs. before spring break, I would say something like...."Hey Bill, will you lose ten pounds before spring break?" Your response would be...."Yes, I will do that." This is now a commitment between you and me only. Depending on our relationship we will say there is a 50% chance you will actually follow through and lose the weight by the designated time. At this point, if you fail on your commitment you will only have to answer to me and feel disappointed in yourself for failing to lose ten pounds by spring break. In order to apply silent committing to greatly improve our chances of success, we must take another step. The conversation will continue something like this....."Hey Jane, Bill just committed to losing ten pounds by spring break. Isn't that fantastic!" Jane would reply, "That's great Bill. I look forward to hearing about your progress". This silent commitment just took our 50% chance of success to 85-90%!! Why? Now Bill knows multiple people are watching and counting on him to make it happen. The more the better when it comes to silent committing.

In that example I silently committed Bill by bringing Jane into the scenario. In order to utilize this tactic on yourself, you must take the steps to bring others into your equation. The best way to begin that process is to share the vision.

3.   Share the Vision

Sharing the vision goes hand in hand with silent committing with an added feature, the breakdown. Once you determine your "superstar" status within and wish to begin making the internal changes that will lead to confidence and trust with yourself, you must share that vision with those you can trust and who will support you. This silent commitment must include the "how's and why's" in order to work properly. Acquaintances and casual friends are not your true support group or the people who will take you where you need to be. The general silent commit works fine for them. Those close to you who will be a great support and anchor need details. You must break down your goals and then break them down again and again until they are so simple and short term it seems silly. When I say break them down I mean actually writing them down with a timeline.

Find people in your life who will challenge you and ask "how" when you share a vision. In my life I have many people who will come to me and say...."I want to be a manager" or "I want to start a business". My first question is "why?" followed by "how?" If someone truly wants to help you they need to know why you are doing something and how you intend on making it happen! I can't help you if I don't understand your intentions, reasons, and how you plan on accomplishing it.

I personally follow my own advice on this daily and I can tell you this is one vital piece of the puzzle you must not leave out. In fact, just the other day I was having lunch with a friend who asked me what I was up to. I proceeded to tell him about this book and that I was going to begin writing that night. At this point I had done some general brainstorming and reviewing of notes, but not told anyone I was going to actually publish this work or when I would begin writing. I took advantage of the simple question "What are you up to?" in order to **silently commit myself** to beginning the process of putting this to paper! Here I am now after midnight typing away....does silent committing and sharing a vision with details work? You better believe it! I will see that same friend this weekend and I'm certainly not going to answer "no" when he asks if I got started as planned.

100% RESPONSIBILITY

Now we will explore a virtue of leadership, as described to me a few years ago by my friends at Team Trek. They refer to this as their "Foundational Virtue". It's called the virtue of 100% Responsibility.

Team Trek explains:

By definition: I am 100% responsible for how I choose to react to what happens to me. Everyone else is 0% responsible.

"Everything can be taken from a man but his freedom to choose. The last of the human freedoms-to choose one's attitude in any given set of circumstances, to choose one's way." Viktor Frankl

Viktor Frankl wrote these words in his book, <u>Man's Search for Meaning</u>. Frankl was a Jewish psychiatrist who discovered this wisdom through his experience as a prisoner in a Nazi concentration camp during World War II. Although Frankl escaped death, he was beaten, tortured, humiliated and restrained in a prison cell. His family, including his wife and children, all lost their lives in the Holocaust.

From this experience Frankl observed that the highest need of a human being is the will to have meaning and purpose in life. In the concentration camps, prisoners who surrendered the will to purpose unto their captors, died shortly thereafter. This led him to the conclusion that human beings find meaning and purpose in life by maintaining the freedom to choose how to react to their external circumstances, no matter how unfair and painful it may be. We choose our own attitude! If we give up the freedom to choose how we will react, we become prisoners to those circumstances emotionally, intellectually, and spiritually.

Responsibility comes from two words, response and ability. This literally means I have the ability to choose my response to what happens to me. I have a free will to choose and NO ONE can cause me to make bad decisions or have a negative attitude without my permission.

100% responsibility means I take responsibility for my own actions and choices. It allows me to be free to choose to do the right thing and be the right kind of person. I do not blame, make excuses, feel sorry for myself, disengage, whine, or rationalize.

Ultimately I have only two choices in life. I can choose to be responsible for my own choices and be free or I can give up that responsibility to my circumstances and become a prisoner or victim of them. How I choose will have everything to do with my behaviors and actions. We are what we think, behaviors are simply the output of thoughts. If we believe others are responsible for how we choose to react (attitude) then we will be a pitiful prisoner or victim of them. If we believe we are responsible for our choices, then we will be free.

The attitude of 100% responsibility does not give us freedom to do whatever feels good, brings us the greatest amounts of pleasure, or avoid the pains of life. It gives us the freedom to do the right thing, be the right kind of person, and live a life of purpose and meaning! Team Trek

Can you be responsible for everything that happens in your

life? Of course not, life is sometimes unfair. Real freedom is being able to respond in the "right" way regardless of the unfair things that may happen to us. There are unique situations which you simply can't control. However, those situations are very rare and you CAN and MUST be 100% responsible for your attitude and how you react in all situations!

I personally like to take the definition above a step further and hold myself 100% responsible for more than just my reaction but also for my behavior or actions prior to the events in my life that may also have influenced the event and outcome.

With that said, I've found over the past few years of application, I have been responsible for nearly every situation when I took the time to examine it further. If you step back and complete a true self-evaluation of the situation, you'll find ownership nearly every time. You may have to look back days, weeks, even years earlier on occasion, but I assure you, every situation you find yourself is related nearly 100% to YOUR choices prior to or during. For example, Hurricane Katrina came upon the Gulf Coast and destroyed nearly everything in her path. She left thousands of families and individuals without power, food supply, water, and gas for weeks. This event hits home with me since I personally have family who still live in that region and were impacted greatly.

What was the situation? Surely I'm not going to say the folks of that region should hold themselves 100% responsible for that disaster correct? The disaster? No! Their situation and circumstances within the disaster? Absolutely!

The disaster was in the hands of the storm......while the

situation was in the hands of every individual living in that region for years prior.

You must understand the difference to grow into a 100% responsible person. Was this the first major hurricane to strike this region? Of course not! In fact, I recall my father telling me stories of Hurricane Camille when I was a small boy growing up in south Mississippi. These stories were usually followed by a lesson on being prepared at all times with things like food storage, water, generators, etc. You see, my father took the attitude of 100% responsibility and took the steps to prepare and teach his children those same lessons to leave a legacy of independence and freedom.

Others took a different path and suffered the consequences as a result. They found themselves in a much different "situation" based on their choices prior to the storm, not the storm.

Now, if we were to interview 100 people that suffered through Hurricane Katrina, how many do you think would say "I was 100% responsible for my situation after the storm passed"? How many would say, "The storm put me in that situation and there's nothing I could do about it?" How many would blame others like the government, the police, National Guard, and anyone else they can think of for their current "situation"? Talk about looking OUTWARD and having 0% responsibility! Which would you say? How many would suffer through the same situation next week if it happened again?

Leaders look to themselves first for accountability and results while followers, or the "sheep", look to others with no personal responsibility. You make the choice!

Ok, hurricanes don't hit home for us all every week so let's dive into an example that is more common. Everyone falls short of a goal at work or during the daily grind from time to time. What most do not realize is when they're confronted by a superior or customer and asked why something failed, the superior or customer would much rather hear them say "I failed by not doing X......I own this and will take the responsibility for correcting it." Rather than hearing them blame someone else or their down line. Sure, many times the failure is down line, but don't you own that as well? Trust me, the superior already knows why the failure occurred in most cases. They're usually more interested in your response and attitude of responsibility. When you pass the buck, you just passed the opportunity to grow and in many cases be considered for promotion in the future!

The attitude of 100% responsibility is a state of mind. True leaders take this approach and it leads to improved choices, better relationships, and a higher level of commitment, 100% of the time!

BUILDING RELATIONSHIPS OF TRUST

Leaders learn the art of gaining influence. Titles, promotions, and success come to those who have already learned how to influence, not the other way around as so many believe.

Influencing others is, in fact, my definition of leadership. That applies to both positive and negative influences in our lives. Many bad people are very good leaders, just for the wrong cause. The key to winning influence is with a simple acronym...BRT.

Building Relationships of Trust is the single most important aspect of growing influence and becoming a strong leader. Think about the people in your life that have influenced you or become a mentor to you. Now think about the "relationship" without any titles associated. I can think of many great mentors and leaders who have influenced my life. Although a few of them had titles such as my "boss", not one of them would I consider anything less than a friend or mentor in whom I fully trust as it relates to that area of my life.

That area of my life? Exactly! I have mentors and people I trust for my physical fitness that I wouldn't invest a single penny into any financial market they recommend. We have to learn to keep the linemen on the line and the running backs in the backfield. I run across this mistake all the time. Uncle Johnny is a great guy and he has always helped me with my relationships and education growing up, so I trust him when he says I should rely solely on my 401K for my retirement. Is Uncle Johnny a good source for my retirement planning when he's having to work until he's sixty five years old and pinch pennies the entire time? While I'm on the subject, I see other sad stories with individuals "blindly" trusting financial advisors (so called). The title DOES NOT give you the expertise or gain my trust.

As Robert Kiyosaki says, "Money doesn't make you rich, knowledge makes you rich."

Great mentors who I allow to influence my life are those that share the education and increase my knowledge, rather than those who would have me just trust them and remain in the dark.

One of my mentors likes to share the story of how he graduated college with a degree in finance and landed his first job as an "advisor" for a well-known company. He recalls how insecure he felt. He even approached his boss and expressed his concern and feeling of inadequacy when speaking with clients. He would ask clients to trust him with millions of dollars, their retirement funds, and savings for their kids' education, yet he had never made more than $35K in a single year! His boss replied, "Just sell them the product!" My mentor quit the job and began his journey to gain true financial education which has been the greatest decision of his life. He now has dedicated his life to exposing these examples and providing education in that arena. His education and marketing enabled him to create a single product that has grossed over 25 million dollars in less than ten years! He now has one of the largest financial newsletters and companies in the market and literally helps educate over fifty thousand people worldwide. Now that is "getting promoted" by following your dreams and a few proven steps.

I tell you his story to illustrate a simple point regarding relationships of trust. Do you think he trusted his "boss"? Why not? Do you think the clients trusted him? Same reason? What was missing? Relationships of trust are not granted based on your title or any other pecking order.

Relationships of trust are built on genuine care and passion for both parties involved, backed by education and results. Fancy power point presentations may fool many people for a while, but eventually the "trust" comes when results come!

Why will I not follow Uncle Johnny into the next investment? Same reason I'm not calling the college grad for financial advice when he's being told to "sell me the product".

All the communication techniques and tactics to win influence in the world can never overcome and win trust if you lack a sincere heart and good character. Using good human relationship fundamentals will even come across as manipulative and insincere without the core foundation built on character.

There are many people in life with great accomplishments and "appear" outwardly to have all that life can offer yet lack "greatness" in their core and primary character. Sooner or later, you will see this expose itself in every long term relationship in their life.

Waldo Emerson once put it, "*What you **ARE** shouts so loudly in my ears I cannot hear what you **SAY**.*"

We have established the importance of ignoring titles (until proven) and keeping the linemen blocking and away from running with the football. Now we must take the necessary steps in our lives to establish that trust that is so important to success in our vision to promote our lives.

1. BUILD

My success promoting so quickly within FedEx Express was attributed to many things. For the ground work, the word **build** in the acronym reminds me of the beginning of that journey. FedEx, like many Fortune 500 companies, are filled with leaders who "climbed the corporate ladder" on their way to the top. Why is this key to the success of these companies?

First, I believe my success at each level was heavily attributed to building talents and success along the way. Mastering the current position in order to build trust from subordinates goes a long way with BRT. Coaching is a key role of all leadership positions with direct and indirect reports. Coaching becomes very difficult when you lack the talent as well. Is it a must to have success at the next level? No. Will it create a smooth ride and speed the process? Yes!

So learn everything there is to learn about every position within your organization along the way. Become the very best at each position you hold and learn all you can about the positions you don't directly hold in your career or field. I recall early in my career with FedEx I was a front line employee holding the position of part-time courier while I finished my college education. I knew I would want to promote if I stayed with FedEx to expand my influence and challenge myself in the future. I started spending my off time with the customer service agents who worked the front counter and research area. Some of my peers thought I was crazy and even asked me why I would spend my time with those employees learning a job I would never hold. I'm not sure I really understood why I was doing it at the time other than I just wanted to learn as much as I could about everything around me. Ironically, within the next year all the employees at that facility reported directly to me, including the service agents. I will never forget the ease of transition with that promotion based on those days I spent learning about every position and "building" the foundation.

2.   RELATIONSHIPS

Relationships are key to success as mentioned **IF** they are managed properly. I recall many years ago having another mentor give me guidance by saying, "Never drink with the boys". What did that mean? He knew I wasn't a "drinker" so why would he say that to me?

Simply put, it means keep the relationships in their proper place! Even when you are peers with a group you must maintain a distance or professional atmosphere that will allow you to one day become their boss. Many aspiring leaders fail in this area and it creates a career road block or what we sometimes refer to as a CLM (career limiting move). Many choose to "let loose" at manager retreats or off-site meetings where the atmosphere is less professional and more like a frat party at times. It amazes me when I see this! Grown men and women with bright futures throwing it away by acting like complete fools. This can happen at all levels and in some cases you may see this unprofessionalism from superiors that will disappoint you and may even tempt you to "join the fun". Don't do it. You don't want to be the topic of discussion around the water cooler the next week. Unless, of course, they are discussing how you remained friendly yet professional at all times.

3.   TRUST

Trust is the glue that holds all relationships together. The word is often used but rarely understood. Many leaders will say "trust but verify" when speaking of subordinates they lead or processes they are managing. Trust that the individual will fulfill the expectations while verifying by checking up on them. I personally subscribe to the reverse approach.....I verify then trust.

You don't gain my trust until you have proven yourself trustworthy. How do you do that? You must first fulfill the expectations or assignments! When you "trust but verify" you really are not having trust in that person. If you did, why the need to verify? Once you've proven to be trustworthy, you gain my trust then I can assign something to you and move on to other important activities without looking back. This is the freedom from having a relationship of trust! If I have to "verify" I'm not truly free and you are not truly trusted.

One example I like to share to illustrate my point is within the movie _A Few Good Men._ Tom Cruise has Jack Nicholson on the stand at one point and is doing his best to extract the truth behind the death of a Marine. At one point Cruise asks Nicholson if he ordered his men to leave the young Marine alone. Jack replies yes he in fact gave the order to leave the Marine alone. Cruise then asks Nicholson if there was a chance that the other soldiers "ignored" the order. Or maybe said, "The old man is crazy" and went ahead with the abuse or the "code red" that killed the young soldier. Nicholson replied, "NOT A CHANCE!" Then continued to explain to Cruise that his men "obey his orders or people die". Cruise then cornered Nicholson when asked if he signed the transfer order to have the young Marine removed from the base. Nicholson, trying to show his concern for the young Marine, said he was having him transferred to "protect him because he was in danger". Cruise wisely reminded Nicholson of his earlier statement about his orders.

"If you ordered them to leave him alone and your orders are always followed or people die.....why the need to transfer and why was he still in danger?"

Of course we all know the rest of the story and how it plays out with one of the classic scenes in movie history. My point, when you have trust in someone else or they trust you, there is no need for "2nd orders" or "verifying". You have a relationship of trust so one commitment is all it takes, then a simple report back process to stay on the same page and ensure an open line of communication for any necessary changes to the original plan. Now take time to consider who you REALLY trust and more importantly, are YOU trustworthy. It is one of the most critical needs for your personal and professional growth.

MASTER THE POSITION YOU HOLD

We live in a world of "I want it now" attitudes. Each generation seems to get a little less patient and with that I see weaker leaders being developed. Whether you are climbing the corporate ladder, running your own business, or simply working on relationships within your network of friends and family, it is crucial you become the very best you can at each position and level you cross.

"Good is the enemy to great!" Julio Melara

Many will make the argument it is not necessary to be the best at a front line position in order to manage that position or lead those people. I agree you don't have to be "**the best**" but rather you do have to be "**your best**" at each.

I have seen many front line employees promote into management positions over the years. Many with a high level of success and others who failed miserably. Those who succeed are known for giving 100% at every job or assignment along the way, no matter how minuscule. Those who fail have many times lost the battle before it ever began. How? You may fool the boss into promoting you into that role but you will never fool those around you who have watched you closely along the way. No one wants to follow a leader who has shown any signs of under-achievement.

Take the time to "master" the position you hold. No job is too small or beneath any of us. If you are currently the person in charge of taking out the trash, then take it out perfectly and without error every time, with your head up and proud to be holding that position! There's nothing worse than someone who accepts a job or assignment and acts as if it is "beneath" them or they are "better than this". If you were "better than this" you wouldn't be DOING THIS!

In addition, there are no tasks beneath great leaders. Back to the football analogy, is the center any less important than the quarterback? Without the center the quarterback will never get the ball. Great leaders find a way to express this to their teams. As a Senior Manager within FedEx, I have had opportunities to move several times to take different positions and operations to lead around the country. Each time in a new market I like to visit each facility I run and "get dirty" with the front line employees right away. I will show up bright and early with the first employees and managers, dressed to get dirty, and jump in the off-load area and get to work. This is the area where brand new employees generally start their career, the grunt work! It's my version of "Undercover Boss" but not quite the same since they generally recognize me. On one such occasion I heard a "click….click" behind me so I turned to see what it was. It was a tenured employee with over 25 years with the company taking pictures of me working "in the trenches" with the brand new employees. I asked her what she was doing and she simply smiled and said, "Never seen that before", referring to someone with my rank and title willing or taking the time out to show them I'm not above the lowest ranking assignment.

Many leaders find this difficult to do. I hear excuses like, "I did my time in those positions and I'm not spending another minute doing that." This resulting in another failed opportunity to win the hearts of the people and gain influence. Pride is an amazing thing….can drive you to the highest levels of success yet can drop you to the lowest of lows just when you allow it to make yourself start believing you are "better than that".

One of my managers recently hired a new employee who he feels is simply not working out. I told him to work with her and report back to me in a week or two as to the progress. He reported back with several stories of disappointment from this individual's attitude and work ethic. I decided I would take the time to watch this employee myself during the evening operation. I noticed everything the manager had been reporting was accurate. The new employee didn't smile, didn't seem to care if they accomplished their goals for the night, and flat out gave attitude to just about anyone who tried to influence her. I was amazed! I couldn't help but remember when I first was applying for jobs and winning opportunities. You couldn't wipe the smile off my face for a month after receiving a new opportunity like that.

I decided to address the issue myself. After a short conversation it was clear she felt "above" the position and task she was assigned. Really? After two weeks you already feel you are better than the task we hired you to do! I reminded her of the interview she completed a few weeks prior where she smiled and was happy to accept ANY job or position. I made it clear she had two choices; stay in that task until she loved it and smiled every day performing it or take a hike! Promoting her to another position would be a cancer to the whole organization at this point. The perception would destroy any chance for her to take a lead role, even if she were ready for it.

Your attitude will determine your altitude in most cases. I have seen leaders gain all the respect and support in the world from their subordinates even though they were not great at a certain position, but rather gave it their best effort and gained the respect from the approach and attitude. Mastering a position is not necessarily becoming the best at the task but rather **UNDERSTANDING** the position and **WHY** it is necessary.

"The person that knows how will always have a job. The person who knows why will be the boss". *Julio Melara*

AVOIDING MY FATHER'S CURSE

"In my experience with leaders and promotions, people generally promote one level beyond their ability to be successful." Dan Tolbert

My father uttered these words to me a very long time ago but they ring in my ears every time I'm promoted or asked to take a new position of leadership. My fear being I would prove him correct one more time!

The theory behind his statement is pretty simple yet profound. I see this over and over as individuals become very successful in their current position, and then all of a sudden their name is being mentioned in meetings discussing future leaders or possible candidates for promotion. I have to remind myself and others a talented and highly successful front line employee may just be all that's there. On the flip side, I have seen average front line employees make outstanding managers and beyond based on their skill set and capacity to team build and lead.

What is the takeaway from this statement? When hiring the next leader in your organization you must ensure you are not being blinded by the record of success in their current position. Analyze the particular skills you need for the position you're hiring for and seek out the candidate that will best fill that position with those skills.

In addition, when building your own skills and seeking the next challenge and promotion, be careful to not fool yourself into thinking your success at the current level will automatically transfer to a new position or role at the next level. There are specific talents and skills to develop at every level. If you fail to reach out and discover those skills, you may just be setting yourself up for failure. This "reaching out" can be a very simple step such as an email or phone call with those who have the knowledge and experience to ensure you understand the skills needed at that next level.

I will share a recent email exchange as the perfect example of this that may help illustrate this simple approach, and share some direct coaching from a Vice President of one of the world's largest corporations! I sent a quick email to David Leech, Vice President Southern Region Operations FedEx Express asking for his thoughts on leadership and specific attributes needed to grow influence and discretionary efforts. I simply told him I was working on a project to help individuals promote their lives and improve their leadership skills. I asked him to share his thoughts on the subject. By asking this, I would receive great coaching AND a very good idea of what it takes to reach that level of leadership.

Dave's response:

"Brandon, I will be interested in hearing about your project next time I am in town.

*I believe the starting point is a person's **integrity** and **moral compass**. **This is the leader's core.** Next would be **passion** and **commitment** to the mission. This is the fuel to develop and support the team's energy. Necessary to overcome the difficult and leverage the success. **Courage** as defined by the ability to access, recognize, tolerate, and appropriately react to risk and opportunity. My experience is the presence of risk/opportunity, often challenges the first* *two characteristic of character or commitment. It leads to a reactionary environment.*

Needed attributes *– to develop teamwork and gain commitment and discretionary effort.*

- **Self Confidence** *– that allows a person to be challenged and build a talented team*

- **Selflessness** *to promote and have others recognized*

- **Technical competency** *to understand the issues, ask the right questions, and provide direction*

- **Work Ethic**

Take care, Dave"

A simple email exchange that probably took less than 30 minutes total from both of us provided great insight, material for me to share with all those I coach, and an improved relationship for future mentoring. One simple example of MANY ways to increase your knowledge, improve your vision, and promote your life.

I believe my father's experience with leaders in his life is a direct result of those leaders failing to reach out and continue their progression as they promote. Never assume you have peaked and are prepared for any challenge! Every growth opportunity provides unique challenges and talents in order to be successful.

As I finished my last few courses prior to graduation from the University of Southern Mississippi I was approached by one of my professors. He asked me one simple question:

"Brandon, what is the most important thing you learned while studying Speech Communication over the last four years?"

I was a bit taken back with such a question. I immediately began trying to remember which courses I had taken from this professor directly to relate those topics in my response in some way to show my gratitude and appreciation for all he had taught me. I honestly could not put my finger on "one thing" I felt stood alone from so many courses taken.

I had no response and decided to actively "listen" to what he would say when I responded with a question in return. I replied, *"Wow, I would have to give that some thought. What do you feel is the most important lesson learned if asked the same question?"*

His response has stuck in my head for many years and I'm grateful for this single conversation, as it has helped me more than he will ever know. He responded, *"The class you took on **LISTENING** is by far the key to developing yourself into a great communicator and key to developing lasting healthy relationships in all areas of life."*

The **art of listening** will be the key to my personal growth? This response seemed so passive. How could such a passive act become so critical to my growth? Over time, I have learned a few keys to listening that have in fact become key to my personal growth with relationships like my marriage as well as my professional growth and success.

The first thing I learned about listening is that it is the *planning* and *preparation* to personal growth. I love working with my son on his baseball swing. I remind him often that the homerun starts with proper stance, body position, bat placement, concentration, and vision. Over 80% of the successful swing (active) depends on these several preparatory steps (passive). Before the first muscle moves and before the ball leaves the pitcher's hand you have determined 80% of the success or failure of that at bat!

So it is with listening in our lives, good listening prepares us for the "swing" and determines over 80% of our success rate.

Another common mistake with listening is the belief that it's just a passive activity. Some believe you join the meeting or conversation, sit there with nothing to do but hear someone speak and move on. Listening when done right is very active. Good listeners are highly active using proper non-verbal cues and especially engaging the brain.

Listening builds relationships of trust more than any other single act. I have struggled with this my entire life. I love my wife for her willingness to forgive me for this as for many years I have "heard" what she was saying but failed to properly "listen" with respect and appreciation for the relationship. Many times she will say, "You didn't hear a word I just said!" My response, "Yes I did!" Then I would repeat her words or general gest of the conversation back to her. What did that tell her? To me, I was able to prove I was listening! To her, I proved I was a jerk! Intentional listening is not always about the knowledge and selfish growth potential, rather it's about the relationship.

I have a friend who is running for State Senate. I recall the first conversation we had about his decision to pursue this position and enter into the world of politics in this way. He asked my opinion and thoughts on whether he should run or not. After informing him we could no longer be friends because I hate politicians we discussed the pros and cons of such a decision and impact on his life and his family. I remember supporting the decision because I felt he had the ability to truly "listen" actively to the people he would serve and take that understanding to action. I didn't concern myself with much more than this characteristic in supporting him. From the first day I met Michael I've been impressed with his ability to actively listen. You feel as if you are the only person in the room and the most important person to him when in conversation. It has served him well and will continue to help him increase his influence and connect with the people he serves.

This is the *art of listening* that will take us from good to great. The only difference in the average and the great ones among us is that the great ones do this ALL THE TIME. It becomes automatic for them. They don't rank personal encounters with levels of importance. They treat everyone equally and eventually everyone notices. Ultimately, growing their understanding, influence, and ability to avoid my "fathers curse".

FINDING MENTORS

If discovery and development of a particular set of skills is vital to your promotion and success, we need to discuss how exactly you discover those skills and begin your development. The best way to do just that is through finding great mentors.

Self-development is limited in many ways. In fact, there really is no such thing as "self-development" if you think about it. You grow from your experiences and improved education. Both tied to others in one way or another. Now we must figure out the best way to tap into resources to improve drastically.

The mentors in my life have literally made the difference every step of the way. I will share my personal experiences with several mentors as I have promoted many times throughout my career and life.

Personal Mentors:

Personal mentors are simply those you allow to influence your personal development throughout your life, not necessarily attached to a specific career or professional role. This begins with family and ends with anyone you allow in your "circle of influence".

My father once had a father/son talk with me about influence and mentors. He may not have known it at the time or even used the word mentor but this conversation, in fact, began my understanding of the importance of mentors. He told me to use my four older brothers as examples in my life. He informed me I was in a unique position being the youngest of five boys. I had the ability to "watch and learn" from them. He specifically told me to "take the good from each of them and throw out the bad" then live my life with that in mind. Of course, I haven't always been successful in doing that but I sure try! I have some amazing older brothers who make it difficult. However, the point remains with me in every relationship and I will illustrate this point several times throughout this topic.

While in college I participated in a study about dress and how it impacts behavior. We found behavior is very closely tied to how individuals were dressing and groomed. Our dress and length of hair impacts our behavior? Absolutely. So what can we learn from that as it relates to our personal mentors?

Just as we clothe ourselves with items that can influence who we become, so it is with our choices of personal mentors. We "clothe" ourselves with friends, family, and others who will ultimately play a key role in how we behave and who we become.

Our personal mentors must have our best interest as the number one contributing force behind their suggestions and coaching for us. My brother Curt is one of my personal mentors. He and I have always been very close as we have grown up. Several times in our lives we have reached out to each other for support and advice. The reason we both fully trust one another and continue to benefit personally from our close relationship is because we know the other has OUR best interest in mind in every way. Although he may not follow the same counsel he gives me at times, he still gives me the counsel he knows will take me to MY VISION and goals for my life. This is the critical ingredient necessary for a personal mentor to be effective. Too often we choose personal mentors based on their accomplishments for THEIR life. As a result, those mentors often counsel with their intentions in mind and fail to counsel properly for what OUR goals may be.

My father was also known for the saying, "birds of feather flock together". This, of course, reminding me to choose good friends that would provide positive influence and growth as well. I have had the opportunity to work with and mentor many youth along the way and 100% of the time......yes, 100% of the time it boils down to the "birds" they are flocking with! Whether they have chosen to flock with those birds based on their comfort zone with them or other reasons, bad behavior is rarely, if ever, solo when it comes to youth.

It is critical that each of us define what personal growth is for our life, then match the mentors with the vision and definition. If your definition of personal growth is flying with eagles, you must ensure you are not being influenced and taught to fly by pigeons!

Professional Mentors:

When it comes to our profession, we must select the proper mentors and choose several. Again, to the point my father made about taking the good from all my older brothers. He didn't say, "Hey, this brother seems to be the best overall so emulate his actions." The key to the counsel was understanding they ALL have good qualities to pull from. Too often I see young aspiring leaders attach themselves to one talented mentor and expect that to take them to the top. It never will....big mistake.

I understood at an early age I had to become something special, something none of my older brothers had become, something that would honor each of them and my parents by becoming one individual with the "good" from all of them. I continue this journey to this day in my life and teach others I mentor they must become better than me to honor me. Never accept walking in my shoes or doing what I have done. Once I have done it, it's no longer special. You must reach the next level. I don't recall who said this, but I love the quote, ***"The extraordinary becomes ordinary at the moment it occurs".*** How true!

I began my career with FedEx as a part-time courier. My first mentor was a horrible leader. In fact, he didn't know he was a mentor to me and still doesn't to this day. I was watching from a distance to learn what I could. I wanted his position, his rank, his influence, his pay, and his future. As I began to study his performance and leadership skills I was sadly disappointed. He treated the employees like garbage, he worked about three hours a day, and couldn't be trusted. I know what you are thinking....I chose him as a mentor? Yes! In fact, he's one of the inspirations and reasons I developed the confidence in myself so quickly and was able to break through the self-doubt that many times holds us back. If he could promote.....I knew I could do it! Funny, but true. In addition, I had to find out why he was in that leadership position and why someone would hire him. I knew he had some keys to my future, regardless of his many faults. I continued to watch and learn. I found out he was amazing when it came to planning. His background was in planning and engineering and it served him well when he was applying for a leadership position in management over many areas that required solid planning. My first professional mentor taught me planning and engineering techniques that I use to this day.

My next mentor was a manager who replaced the first. Ironically, this mentor was what many call a "people person" and had the ability to connect with every single employee. It was the direct contrast to what I had experienced with the first. A fresh take on my experience. This mentor had great communication, made time for everyone, had the donuts in the morning, and knew every employee's name and even their spouse, etc. I absolutely loved being around him and learning from his character and leadership style. He had a saying, "Keep it Positive!" I heard that said in our workplace a thousand times if I heard it once. It was contagious and uplifting. Just what the doctor ordered from the previous planner who didn't care to know your name. However, Mentor #2 had some weakness that began to show. It wasn't until he transferred to another facility that this became an issue. Our facility was filled with top performers who always did a good job. The new facility he went to manage had some serious employee performance issues. Their performance as a facility was among the worst in the District. My Mentor #2 struggled in a big way trying to reverse the trend and improve the performance. They literally took his kindness for weakness, and it ultimately resulted in his failure as a leader there. His kindness was not a weakness. On the contrary it was one of his greatest strengths. However, his inability to "kindly" remove the cancer from the organization by holding them accountable was his weakness.

The next several mentors in my path were higher level mentors with very few flaws. Mentor #3 was the man who hired me into my first management position. I took many things from this mentor and still learn from him to this day on a personal level since he's semi-retired. He will never truly retire from his influence as a leader. He taught me you can and must become a great leader in all aspects of life. He helped me understand leadership is about influence not the title. In fact, if leadership equated to titles, his title would have been ten feet long! I learned winning the hearts and minds of the people would elevate my success and my career faster than anything else. He put the talents of Mentor #1 and Mentor #2 together and left out the bad. He taught me to manage processes and lead people. Warren will always be a personal and professional mentor, not to mention one of my closest friends.

Interestingly, Mentor #3 promoted me into the position vacated by Mentor #2 and then I soon found myself being assigned to manage the facility that exposed Mentor #2's weakness. Welcome to the party right!

I will never forget my first day walking into that facility. I had checked into the hotel the night before and done some research on the performance of that team. I had broken down the key areas of opportunity and realized the performance couldn't get much worse, so I felt pretty good about my chances to make a difference. I got up bright and early and made my way to the facility expecting the worst. I walked in and what was the first thing I saw plastered on the wall? "Keep it Positive!".....I smiled and went to put my stuff in the office when I noticed about three more "Keep it Positive" signs and banners. I began to miss Mentor #2 a bit from seeing the signs. It reminded me of all the good times and how much I learned from him and respected him as a real "people person". I continued out to the operation where I would meet the 50 or so employees and introduce myself for the first time. I fully expected a hornet's nest of disgruntled employees from hell! I was shocked at the reality. These employees were very nice and friendly. They were supportive with the exception of a very few. I spent that first day just introducing myself and preparing them for the meeting the next day that I would have before work began.

The next morning I set the alarm for about one hour earlier to ensure I was the first person to arrive at the facility. My first order of business was to remove all signs and banners that said or referred to "keeping it positive". I replaced those signs with graphs and ranking charts clearly showing the employees how they ranked compared to the other 20 or so facilities within the District. Yes, they were pretty much the bottom of the barrel in every aspect. The employees arrived prepared for the meeting. The first question asked was "Where's the donuts?".....followed by, "What happened to all the signs?". I began my meeting by once again introducing myself followed by reminding them what we are in business to do. I reminded them we are a service company that must serve the customer while maintaining profitable returns......that's what we are paid to do. Success is defined by those two things! I then showed them specifically how this team is failing miserably in both categories. Therefore, the "Keep it Positive" signs have been removed and replaced with "reality" signs. The reality that we are failing and it must change immediately. I followed this by answering the second question..."There are no donuts until we do our part in contributing to the company's ability to turn a profit to pay for them". I then outlined my expectations for each of them to remain employed and on this team. You could hear a pin drop in that meeting. I ended with my belief in them and my determination to help them get there. I told them I know they can be at the top of those charts if they choose. I then broke it down for them so they could see exactly what effort and improvements would be needed to go from the bottom to the top. They saw if they worked together, it could happen quickly. And it did. Mentor #3 taught me real success comes with balance.

Mentors #4, 5, 6, and beyond have all had multiple talents yet areas I will discard. This is the key....learn from my father and have multiple mentors. Take the good....leave the bad and never discard anyone based on their areas of weakness. We all have talents and nearly every mentor you choose will add value to your life if used properly.

BUILDING YOUR NETWORK

Building a network will take you out of your comfort zone and into relationships that can produce significant contributions in your life and to your success. Many confuse mentors with their network. Although your mentors may be part of your network, your network must reach much farther than just your group of mentors.

When describing a network, I like to share the example of my personal network as it relates to my home. A few years ago I moved my family to Georgia. When deciding to make the move from Austin to Atlanta I knew I needed a "mentor" or two in my search for a home to buy. Then I would need a "network" to ensure we continued to be happy and successful living in our new home.

My first mentor was a relative who had lived in the area for several years and had many of the same goals for her family as I had for mine. I trusted in Amy's advice and knew she would lead me in the right direction as it related to school zones, recreation, shopping, safety, and quality areas for us to raise our kids. My mentor gave me the direction and ensured I was prepared for the decision and prepared for success.

Now I had to build my "network" to ensure continued success in living in Georgia. First, we needed a trusted stone mason to build our outdoor fireplace and other concrete work. After some research and interviews, we met Hugo. I hired Hugo to complete the fireplace work first and once I saw the amazing work his company performed, I hired him for a few other jobs. I then needed a carpenter for some finishing work in the basement. Hugo introduced me to three potential candidates. We chose one and have been very pleased with the work. Then I needed a plumber to complete an additional bathroom. A manager who worked for me referred a friend named Hugh. Hugh has done all of our plumbing since and has referred our current AC/Heating guy among others. As you can see, we currently have a network of many individuals covering all areas of need. Any issue that may arise in our life, I have someone in our network on speed dial.

This personal network can be used as a template for your professional network. I have built a network twice the size of my personal network for my professional goals and career. I will share one example. Several years ago I was asked to be part of a Corporate Communication Advisory Board. Taking this assignment meant traveling to meet with other leaders from around the country to discuss and advise our communication department as it related to messaging the directives of the company to thousands of employees and managers. Every member of that Board did a great job participating and continue to add value to this day. In addition to the task at hand, I found this to be another great opportunity to grow my network. I have made several contacts and grown my network from this group. By paying close attention and making note of the talents and expertise each brought to the team, I found leaders with talents and abilities I could certainly use and learn from. By simply adding them to my network and developing relationships, I have been able to tap into their talents over the years to improve my own performance and leadership. In addition, I have been able to assist them in return and develop additional resources as a result.

Building a grand network with no end is critical on our journey to find our potential. Use your mentors to prepare yourself for the role and assist in charting your path. Then build a grand network of support for ALL areas of need. Your success will be determined by your choice of mentors and your ability to build a large network of supporting individuals and groups around you. Circle, highlight, put stars next to, or whatever you need for this paragraph! I can't stress enough how important it is to engage great mentors and have a network of experts to step in when needed.

GAINING EXPERIENTIAL KNOWLEDGE

Spring training has arrived! Its spring time and Billy is now a freshman in high school. Football practice with the "big boys" is about to commence with uncertainty and a bit of fear needing to be addressed. Billy is transitioning from being the "top dog" on the field as the 8th Grader to joining the varsity squad and now being one of the smallest and inexperienced on the field. This promotion could be a painful one!

Billy is trying out for the position of outside linebacker on the varsity team. "Linebackers! Come with me", shouts Coach. Ten players run to follow Coach away from the rest of the team. Today is the first day of practice in full pads, a day every freshman dreads as they will undoubtedly become targets for the older boys to "welcome" them to the team.

"Its popcorn time boys", shouted Coach. "Time to see what you are made of and send the pretenders home", added the largest returning senior in the group with a smile. "Make one line facing me and tighten up those chin straps", directed Coach. Coach then called Sam to come to him and turn to face the line of players about ten yards away. "Now, at the sound of my whistle I need each of you to run full speed at Sam and put him on his butt! The first one to put Sam on his butt will get the prize for the day and not have to run sprints", said Coach. It should be noted, Sam was the returning three year starter at inside linebacker. He had every division one school recruiting him and had just a week prior squatted over 650 lbs. for all to see. He was huge, fearless, and by the look in his eyes couldn't wait for someone to even try to knock him down!

Billy was about six players from the front of the line as the drill began. The whistle blew! The first player took off full speed toward Sam. From the sound of the contact it was now clear to Billy why this drill was called Popcorn! Sam took the hit and threw the other player to the ground like he was a cheerleader on the wrong field. The whistle blew again, the next took off and did his best to apply the punishment to Sam, with little success. The whistle continued to blow and all the players took their best shot at Sam. After the last player hit, Sam yelled "Is that all you got!" Billy hit Sam with all he had and it was like running into a brick wall. Self-doubt began to increase as Billy began to come to grips with the fact he would be standing their alone in a matter of minutes with guys like Sam trying to destroy him.

"Next!" yelled Coach. A sophomore named Steve ran to Coach and turned around while hitting himself in the head as to get pumped up and ready. "Come on!" shouted Steve. The first whistle blew and Steve took the first hit and got ready for the next. Second whistle, then third, then on the fourth Steve got blasted and hit the ground on his back side! "Get up!" screamed Coach. The whistle blew again and again and Billy among the others just kept pounding Steve, knocking him down several times. This was clearly not a fun event for Steve or anyone unprepared.

The third player took his turn. Tony was a veteran being in his senior year yet still a smaller guy, not much bigger than Billy. Tony confidently took to his position and the whistles began. Tony was taking the hits and somehow maintaining his position while delivering some punishment of his own. Billy was amazed and now hopeful! As soon as Tony finished, Billy grabbed Tony and said, "Help me out man. How did you do that?" Billy knew Tony had something of value to offer and he needed it fast!

"Two things, stay low and get off first" said Tony. Tony explained the low man wins and so does the one who decides to hit first. Billy digested that for a second. Stay low and be the aggressor! "Billy, you are up!" yelled Coach. Billy stepped into position, chin strap tight, mouth piece in, and heart pounding. The whistles began and here they came, one after another. Billy staying low and doing his best to hit first was holding his position well through the first seven guys. Then came Sam. BOOM!! Sam dropped Billy on his butt! Seeing stars and trying to get up quickly Billy had never felt such an impact in his football life! Jumping up just in time to get the last few hits, Billy recovered and finished the drill.

Tony approached Billy after the drill and said, "You had it! Why did you not attack Sam like the others?" It became apparent to Billy that he had allowed Sam to be the aggressor. Why? Did he lack the courage or just saw the monster coming and didn't attack as he had the previous teammates out of uncertainty of the outcome? Either way, Billy ended up on his butt!

This infuriated Billy who felt he missed an opportunity to impress the coaches and live up to his potential. Billy felt he had to do something. Not sure what, he decided to confront the lion head on! Billy walked over to Sam while they were standing on the side waiting for the next drill. "That won't happen again" said Billy. "WHAT!" shouted Sam. "What did you say to me!" he continued. Billy now in an uncomfortable position, not wanting to make a big deal of it, but definitely wanting to send a message didn't expect the outburst from

Sam. "No disrespect Sam, but just wanted to say good job out there but also needed to tell you it won't happen again", replied Billy. Sam yelled, "Coach, we have ourselves a rookie freshman talking trash over here saying I can't put him on his butt again!" Coach replied, "Great! Let's go boys, follow me!"

"What have I done", Billy thought. "Line up!" Coach said as he prepared his whistle. "Billy, to the front....Sam to the back!" he continued. This meant Sam would get the last hit on Billy after the others had done their best to soften him up! Tony got Billy's attention just before the start and said, "You took his best shot already, now attack him like the rest."

Billy strapped up and bit down on his mouthpiece trying to mentally prepare for the drill again. Looking down just before the first whistle blew, Billy saw his hands made into fists and it took him back several years to the boxing match with his cousin James. Clinched fists, Billy knew the outcome was in his hands and it started with overcoming the mental battle going on in his head. Stay low, hit first, attack them! The whistle blew! Billy began shedding one after another, even easier than the first time. Then came Sam, who appeared to start running from much farther back this time. POW!! Billy being knocked back a few feet stumbled but kept his feet and stayed upright. Sam tried to finish the job with a second hit and grab of the jersey. Billy fought back grabbing Sam's face-mask and pushing up to do his best to keep Sam off him. They tussled for a few seconds ending with Coach breaking them up and reminding them "We are a team, now stop fighting". Sam glared at Billy as Billy said, "Didn't happen" and proudly walked away.

Every linebacker in the drill gave Billy the look of "nice job" with Tony giving a jumping high five! "I told you!" said Tony.

What can we learn from Billy's experience? First, experiential knowledge comes in multiple forms. As the "rookie" on the team and first experience with practice at that level, Billy had no **personal** "experiential knowledge" to learn from. However, did Billy have experiential knowledge to learn from? Of course he did. It made the difference between Billy's initial experiences through the drill compared to Steve. Steve got knocked down several times and punished through the entire drill while Billy held his ground and only got knocked down one time. Billy took the time to reach out to Tony. Billy saw Tony as a mentor or someone who had experience in the drill and wasn't afraid to ask, "*Help me out man, how did you do that?*" Had Steve tapped into Tony's or anyone else for their previous experience in the drill, he would have also had an advantage.

As mentioned previously, mentors are key in all areas of your progression in life. Mentors have a wealth of knowledge and many personal experiences for you to learn from. Following Billy's example by "reaching out" will drastically improve your performance and experiences throughout your progression.

Does secondary experiential knowledge solve all the problems and eliminate the need for personal experience? Absolutely not, but it's a key step many fail to utilize in all walks of life. Where did secondary experiential knowledge stop and personal start for Billy? Tony's previous experience helped Billy get through the first drill with technique. Billy was only able to conquer Sam AFTER gaining first-hand experience. It took Billy getting knocked down by Sam to FEEL the hit from the best in the game. Once Billy felt it, and Tony reminded him he had *"taken his best shot"*, he was then able to gain the mental toughness and confidence to attack Sam and reach his potential for the day. When I hear people say they learned lessons the "hard way", I like to remind them in most cases that was by their choosing.

Experience **is** one of life's best teachers. However, too often people think they have to rely solely on their personal experiences for their progression. I have a brother who has been a great example for many of us in our lives. David is famous in our family for saying, "I don't need to feel the pain of my own experience if I can learn from watching you suffer from the bad choice." How true. The ole' putting your hand into fire to know it burns scenario.

In our quest to reach our full potential and promote our lives, we must take time to learn from other's experiences in addition to gaining personal experience.

Now allow me to share another very common experience to illustrate the importance of personal experiential knowledge. In my professional career I often find myself looking to hire and promote leaders. I'm often disappointed with answers to behavioral questions I ask my candidates. Most business owners or decision makers in corporations want to know what behavior they can expect from their potential leaders. We can't afford to hire you and HOPE you represent the company or business properly when thrown into the situations of running the business. We use situational questioning to get an idea of the behavior we can expect to see when placed in similar situations.

Take every opportunity to gain personal experience by volunteering to cover your mentors when they are on vacation or act as them while they are close by to help coach. Place yourself in unfamiliar territory and uncomfortable situations as often as possible. All these experiences will come back to reward you many times over and guarantee your success in promoting and elevating your life.

If you find yourself afraid of these situations, you are probably human. The fear of failure or fear of others judging you are real and common. You must find the courage to overcome those fears and gain the experiential knowledge that will take you to new heights. I don't want to hear "I would do this" when I ask you a situational question. I want to hear "I have had a similar situation and this is **WHAT I DID**." Without reaching out to learn from others and find opportunities for those experiences, you will have no acceptable answer and NO promotion!

APPLYING FOR THE POSITION

Now let's dive into specific nuts and bolts of applying for positions of promotion for your professional progress. In the new era of technology it's simply not as easy as it once was. Typing up a resume and walking into a potential employer to hand deliver, while hoping to meet the boss is simply no longer the case. Many promotions and new careers are started now through online searches and using the web as a tool to further your career. There are many helpful sites and links to support your education of online application and applying for positions via the internet. Here are a few tips to remember while using this method:

Before you start looking for jobs and completing online job applications, you'll need an updated version of your resume ready to upload. You may also need a cover letter to apply for some jobs.

Make sure your resume includes your current contact information and work history. Save your resume as yournameresume.doc, rather than with a generic file name like "resume" so the hiring manager will connect **you** with the **resume** when they review it.

Have a basic cover letter ready that you can customize for each job you apply for.

Some sites let you upload an existing resume from Microsoft Word on your computer with the click of a button. On other sites, you may need to copy and paste from your resume into an online profile or use a resume builder that is incorporated into the job application system.

Have the details of your employment history ready. Online application systems typically ask for the same information as paper job applications including your contact information, educational background and employment history including job titles, starting and ending dates of employment, and salary for each position.

Create a list of job search keywords that reflect your interests - location where you want to work, type of position, industry, type of career, etc. This step will save you countless hours of search.

Some job boards and company websites require users to create an account when they apply for jobs. It's a good idea to start your online job search by creating an account on at least one of the major job boards including Monster, CareerBuilder, and Dice for tech jobs. If you're seeking a professional position, it's also important to create a profile on LinkedIn.

In addition to using a job board, using a job search engine can save you a lot of online job search time. For example, LinkUp searches for jobs only on company websites, so all the listings you get will be current openings. Indeed.com searches jobs on job boards, newspapers, associations, and company web sites, including most of the Fortune 1000 companies. SimplyHired also searches across the Internet for jobs.

When you use a job search engine, you can search for jobs all in one place, rather than having to visit all these sites independently. Search using the job search keywords list you created and you'll get a list of job openings that match your specifications very quickly. When you click on a job opening, you'll get instructions on how to apply and/or be directed to a company website to apply.

Whether applying in person or using the tools I've just shared, the key to the application process is accuracy and honesty. Many are tempted to use the resume or application process as a way to "inflate" their actual experience or capabilities. Never allow this to happen! It will only be exposed in the interview process and you will lose trust and further opportunity.

I recommend my readers visit the below website for further coaching on this subject. Many of the keys and thoughts I share are directly from education from this source and others that are linked to it. A perfect example of using a "network" to help. I have never applied for or searched positions or career opportunities online but it's clear to see it has become the present and future for job seekers or those looking for a better career.

http://jobsearch.about.com/od/jobapplications/u/job-applications.htm

(http://jobsearch.about.com/od/jobapplications/u/job-applications.htm)

http://www.indeed.com/headhunters

Applying internally for promotion within your current employer is often similar to the online application process previously described. Large corporations generally have their internal site to visit for career opportunities and a specific application process. I refer anyone in this situation to seek support from the support staff provided. These applications must be exact in order to qualify for the position. One single error in many cases will disqualify you before you get past the very first step. My point, don't "go it alone" as they say. Spend the time to read every word of the process provided and study the specific needs to apply. Prepare your application packet then have multiple support staff, including mentors, review the packet and provide feedback. This packet is your first impression in many cases. It must be in line with the message you wish to send.

I personally enjoy reviewing packets for potential candidates I'm preparing to interview. Although I may ask for a laundry list of facts, history, and details about work experience; the letter of intent often paints the entire picture for me. This is a simple letter I require of each candidate which explains who they are and why they feel they deserve a shot at the promotion. When you take the time to see the big picture as to WHY you are being asked to submit a particular item, it will help you to "paint the picture" and potentially get an interview.

INFORMAL INTERVIEWS

While studying Speech Communication at the University of Southern Miss, I had the pleasure of taking a course on interviewing. I recall the first day of class and the very first lesson taught on the subject. The first day "changed my mind" about interviews and it has crossed my mind nearly every day since!

What was taught on day one that made such an impact? I recall walking into the class and having the professor greet each student with a hand-shake and welcome, followed by a quick question that went something like, "What do you hope to get from this course?" I don't exactly recall my answer to the professor, probably something sarcastic like "My needed credit to graduate." Whatever the answers we were giving, they were not well thought out or delivered with any intent to impress. Very few put their best foot forward with the quick response as we each were just looking to get to a seat and begin the class.

The professor then began class by saying, "Each of you have just completed your first test and failed miserably!" "What the heck is going on?" I thought. "Each of you were just interviewed and I must say, I'm not impressed", said the professor. What was he talking about? An interview is when you get dressed up in your best outfit and go meet with the boss or a group of interview panel members and answer questions about the job or promotion you are seeking, right? **Wrong**. Our first lesson was to shatter our preconceived notions about what an "interview" looked like.

The professor spent the next semester helping us understand nearly every interaction we have are in fact, interviews. Many years later, it makes more sense to me as I'm constantly on the search for potential leaders. Even the simplest conversations I have about sports or completely unrelated subjects are in fact "interviews" with those individuals. I find myself watching their body language, attitude, and passion they bring to the subject. Many of the leaders I have promoted over the years were 75% PROMOTED before the formal process ever started. They crossed so many bridges and answered so many of my questions and concerns about their character, passion, leadership, and integrity through simple non-formal interviews, the formal interviews became nearly irrelevant.

I will share an experience that illustrates the power of "non-formal" interviews. My wife and I enjoy going to a specific restaurant that allows us to bypass the wait list and sit directly in front of the cooking area. These seats are not the quiet and romantic corner table with candlelight but they provide some entertainment generally not available at a restaurant. The entertainment? We get to watch the cooks working at their amazing pace, along with witnessing the process used to interact with waiters and managers. In addition, we get to see nearly every dish prepared just a couple feet away, which usually gives us ideas of what to order.

On one occasion, we were sitting directly in front of the pizza cook using the wood burning fire. This young man was working at a pace we'd not seen from anyone prior. He was moving back and forth from the ingredients section, to the oven, to the pasta section, then back with precision! I leaned over to my wife and said, "Check this kid out." After watching him for a few seconds my wife replied, "You are going to offer him a job aren't you." "Maybe! I need to interview him first", I replied with a grin! So the interview began.

A little small talk ensued and within five minutes I learned he was recently married, had one child on the way, how long he had worked for this restaurant, his desire to pursue a career in leadership, his understanding of teamwork, and probably most importantly his enthusiasm and desire to learn and develop himself with an attitude of 100% responsibility.

Needless to say, he was "promoted" into my organization within two weeks! His pay doubled and his opportunity to progress into the leadership career he dreamed of became a reality. From dead end job to immediately doubling his income and endless opportunity, all based on one single encounter of a non-formal interview.

This example is just one of many I could share. This was a great example of a positive experience and outcome. The examples of negative impressions and lost opportunities are, unfortunately, more of the norm. Always consider this example and the lesson taught by my professor as you go about your daily life. Someone is truly always watching and you are constantly in the middle of non-formal interviews.

WINNING THE FORMAL INTERVIEW

The formal interview is in most cases the climax of the promotion process. This 30-90 minute event will determine who receives the offer versus who is rejected. As described previously, every promotion in your life has the ability to change your life financially, mentally, spiritually, and physically forever.

Once I get down to the top five to ten candidates through the application review and qualification process, ALL of the remaining candidates have a very real chance at winning the promotion and changing their life. It then boils down to the formal interview. One of the most disappointing experiences I have had to endure over the years is watching individuals fall apart in the formal interview. Let's discuss some specifics to ensure YOU always win once you get the chance to formally interview.

Prepare:

Most organizations will provide some direction as to what to expect and how to prepare physically for the actual interview. You may be given specific instructions on dress code, types of questions to expect, presentations to prepare, or other specifics pertaining to the organization.

This first step is the first opportunity to begin to distance yourself from the others in the competition. Never make the mistake of thinking you are "in the lead" going into an interview. Most hiring managers or owners looking for the next individual to add to their organization or promote within are entering the formal interview looking for one candidate to emerge the clear winner.

Every candidate will receive the same welcome communication and instructions to prepare. What will you do that the rest will not think to do? Are you going to go spend $1,000.00 on a new suit to do your best to impress? I hope not! That would just tell me you struggle at making sound financial decisions.

One of the most important and often overlooked keys to winning in a formal interview is the mock interview. Any mentor worth their salt will ensure you prepare with several mock interviews but you can't leave it up to them, 100% responsibility right! The mock interview will help you clear several hurdles. First, you must get a mentor or team of mentors to support this process. Ask those who have interviewed for similar positions or mentors who interview others for similar positions to put you through a mock interview. This is not just to go through the motions, but to actually make it as real and difficult as possible.

For those I mentor, I will prepare very similar questions to what they may be asked in the real interview. We then ask multiple other people to help by joining in the mock interview and take notes about their impressions and thoughts as the interview proceeds. If your mentor can get someone to join in the mock interview that you don't even know, that is ideal. The more difficult the mock interview, the easier the real interview will be.

Practice over and over again. I had an MMA coach who used to remind me of this by saying, "Train hard - Fight easy!" How true! This advice applies to all walks of life. You must put the work in during the preparation stages to win the real competition. This key principle must be taught to our children at the earliest ages. This is keeping them "old school" as we learned from Coach Bowden in the beginning. My son Coleman is playing baseball for the first time. He is five years old and playing in the league where many of the kids are just learning the basics of baseball. It becomes very evident which parents are working with the kids at home versus those who expect to sign them up and have the coach teach them everything. As we began the year I was asked to help coach. I had planned on holding off on coaching until ALL the kids playing had a clue. My plan was around age eight or nine but clearly that plan failed miserably. Back to the point, these kids are very coachable at this stage so I was actually encouraged and felt I made the right decision to help coach these young kids. I began working individually with them at practice and helping them see some basics that would drastically improve their performance. After practice, I would sometimes grab a parent and describe what they could do at home to help speed up the process and improve their son's performance on the field. It's pretty clear when they take the advice and we can see the change immediately the next practice or game.

Since this past summer leading up to my son's first year of baseball I have been taking him to the park and working drills with him. The whole time explaining to him that we are "putting in the work" now so he can be the best when the season comes. Once we started practice he noticed a significant difference in his skills versus the other kids. After the first practice I asked him if he wanted to stay after everyone else went home and take some ground balls and hit a few more rounds. He replied, "Yes!" We stayed late that night and literally were the last two people at the park well after dark. Just before we finished I brought him to me and knelt down beside him and said, "Son, take a look around. What do you see?" He replied, "No one else is here." I explained, "That's right, if you will always be the first one on the field and the last one off, you will always be the best! You see, the other kids are home playing video games while their dads are watching television or surfing the internet. We will always beat them when it's game time!"

I knew he got the message when the next practice day came and he asked how early we would leave and asked me to explain to mom that we would be staying late again past his bedtime. When the team practice ended I heard him telling another kid on the team, "We are staying after to **put some work in**....you want to stay with me and my dad?" Now my son is influencing others at age 5. Not just the kids but the parents as well.

Just as "putting in the work" for my son equates to home-runs and victories come game time, so will putting in the work prepare you for the formal interview and success promoting your life. Practice....Practice.....Practice!! Never forget the upcoming 30-90 minute event has the potential to change your life! Is it worth hours or days of practice?

I also like to refer to the Olympic athletes to compare. They train their whole lives for a 2 minute event! If they fail to reach their goal, they have to wait another 4 years to attempt to reach their goal again. If we would treat all our goals as if we were Olympians with a similar timeline, I believe we would achieve at a much higher rate. Our more frequent timelines of opportunity are blessings but can also be a curse if we allow them to hinder our passion and intensity level during the preparatory process.

Proper communication pre-interview is another key in creating separation. I have found most candidates receive my interview invitation and simply show up at the appointed time and place. What's wrong with that? Isn't that what the instructions direct them to do? Sure it is, and there's nothing "wrong" with that if you don't have a desire to begin to win the promotion at the earliest possible points! As explained previously, ALL communication is in fact an interview in process. So when you receive a letter or communication from a potential employer, doesn't it deserve a response? It amazes me every time I send out 5-10 letters offering an interview to individuals that will literally change their lives forever and I receive 2-3 responses saying "Thank you". Take time to send that simple thank you and mention your excitement to meet with them. Consider the people who are taking time out of their busy schedules to provide you with this opportunity, and then thank them for it. This is not just good practice to begin separating yourself from the pack but also just plain and simple good manners.

Reaching out to key players is the next step in preparing for the interview. Research the organization and find the individuals that are key to the organization, then contact them directly by phone or in person if applicable. Each of these calls or discussions are in fact mini-interviews as well so take them serious and prepare what questions you will ask ahead of time.

For example, I have engineers, human resource staff, safety specialists, and many other support staff working in my organization. In addition, there are other leaders and managers who report directly to me. Do you think I receive feedback on candidates who reach out to these individuals prior to the interview? Of course I do! These "mini-interviews" are critical to your chances at the promotion. I don't know any hiring manager or boss who wants to disrupt their organization by bringing in someone who does not connect with their current staff. In fact, many of the candidates I have rejected over the years were turned down more for my belief they were simply not a good fit for my organization, not necessarily that they were not qualified for the position. Leadership is about influence not titles, reaching out to the support staff ahead of time and beginning to influence them in your behalf is a very strong start and may be the difference between the offer or rejection.

Visit the organization if applicable. Many promotional opportunities require a move to a new area, report to a new department, or join a new group. Your ability to win in the formal interview may be greatly enhanced by visiting the organization prior. This key step must be handled properly or it will work to your demise. Here are a couple of things to remember when attempting a visit.

First, contact the hiring manager or boss prior to the visit to gain his or her permission to visit the organization. Explain your intentions to visit simply to get a visual of the organization and possibly meet and greet some key players. If approved, ask the hiring manager for a contact to work out the visit logistics and work with directly. Most will provide you with a key player in their organization who will give you the tour of the facility or organization. Reach out to this individual in advance and ensure they understand how much you appreciate their time and willingness to help.

Prior to arriving, do your homework on the organization or facility. If you can run their performance numbers or get access to any information about them specifically, have that information in mind when touring the organization. Once you arrive to visit, remember you will be under a microscope at all times within the organizational visit. Employees and staff will want to know who you are, why you are there, and what your intentions are for their future. Stay positive and polite. Take time to meet as many individuals as possible, complimenting everything possible.

Take notes! As you visit take mental notes that will determine your responses to questions you receive in the formal interview. It is ok to have a pen and pad of paper to take notes in some cases, but I suggest avoiding that if possible. Having someone walk around with a note pad of paper and pen taking notes is generally not well received. If you have a hard time remembering specifics, have a very small pad of paper that will fit in your pocket and only take it out to write a quick reminder note then hide it back in your pocket to avoid the perception previously mentioned. These notes should be both positive and document areas of opportunity for improvement that you see. Again, point out the positive to your escort and others but keep the opportunities for improvement to YOURSELF! Criticizing the performance or organization in any way will be a major mistake and most likely cost you the promotion. Be patient, you will have your opportunity in the formal interview to discuss the potential improvements you find with the right people.

Finish the visit process with a thank you note to all those involved in making this visit possible, including the hiring manager. A simple note saying something like, "Thank you for allowing me to visit your organization. I met some amazing people and saw some great things. I look forward to discussing what I experienced further when we meet for the interview." Simple, to the point, yet leave them with the thought you have something else to share or offer from the visit. This will help open the door to that discussion in the formal interview, something not available to those who fail to make the pre-interview visit.

Arriving to the interview is the next step in the preparation process. If interviewing in an unfamiliar place or city, take time the day before or at least hours before the interview to drive to the location. This will create familiarity with the area and ensure you are not running late or get lost when it counts.

Once you arrive for the formal interview, ensure you follow the instructions given prior, exactly as given. Do not deviate or attempt to "impress" by going outside the given direction at this point. Arriving extremely early is one of the most common mistakes I see in this process.

Normally, arriving early is a good thing right? In this process, you are given a specific time for a reason and deviating may interrupt the plans and result in a negative outcome. For example, if you arrive extremely early (over 1 hour) you will most likely end up sitting in a waiting area with the candidate(s) assigned to interview before you. Although this situation is not the end of the world, it's simply not professional and may result in putting yourself and the other candidates in an awkward position just minutes prior to your most important interview. You must enter that interview with a sound and confident mind to perform your best. Meeting your competition and spending the last hour of preparation time socializing and trying to "feel out" your competition could be detrimental to your interview performance.

Allow me to share another personal experience that relates. When I was in my early twenties I applied for a management position in Denver, CO. My application and qualifications enabled me to receive an interview invitation. I was extremely excited as you can imagine. This was my first attempt at promoting into a management position, which would change my life drastically and kick-start my career in leadership. At my age and very short tenure with the company, I was surprised to receive the interview invitation for a position in a part of the country I had no real network or connections.

Excited and now with improved confidence, I worked my way through the preparation process and flew to Denver a day early. I followed the steps outlined above by visiting the location I would be managing. As I met with personnel and reviewed the operation, my confidence grew stronger and I knew I was the "man for the job." There was no doubt in my mind this was my job and the place I would begin my career in leadership.

The interview day came and I was up early and decided I would make my way downtown to the offices where I was to interview with at least 90 minutes to spare. My plan was to arrive early, sit in a quiet place and review my notes, mentally preparing for the most important event in my young career. Big mistake!

I arrived as planned, found a quiet place to sit and began reviewing my notes. Within a few short minutes the room began to fill with suits. Several other candidates arriving early to interview. They were all talking and socializing since they all knew each other very well. I suddenly found myself the "lone wolf" from the other side of the Country. I didn't know any of these men or women. I couldn't help but listen in on their conversations and do my best to "size up" the competition. A few of them were speaking about their relationship with the hiring manager. They were talking about projects they had worked on within the hiring manager's organization and how they really enjoyed building those relationships. In addition, I couldn't help but notice I was probably 15 years younger than anyone in the room. My level of confidence began to sink! Doubt began to enter my mind and my focus shifted from where it should have been. Rather than focusing on my notes and presenting what I bring to the table, I was beginning to consider ways I could overcome the disadvantages I "thought" I was facing.

As a result, I probably didn't interview as strongly as I could had I just avoided that situation altogether. I was not selected for that position, however, I did receive a note from the hiring manager post interview asking me to apply for the next position she would have available soon. She informed me she had hired a local candidate simply based on her knowing a little more about him. She continued with letting me know I had interviewed very well but not done enough to separate myself from the successful candidate. As an outsider, you must create enough separation in the interview to provide the interviewer with enough confidence to take a chance with the unknown.

This was a great experience for me personally and professionally. I realized I had placed the doubts in my mind and created obstacles that simply did not exist in the minds of others involved. Had I just stayed focused on presenting myself and my talents, I know I would have separated myself in that interview.

The bottom line, YOU are the only one placing limits on yourself! Never play the victim or create doubt that should not be in your mind at any point of your progression.

Now let us explore the greeting and interview. Generally, there will be someone to greet you and provide you with a place to wait to be called back. Remember, your interview begins the minute you walk through the door and greet this person. A little known fact, these people are watching you and they love to tell the decision makers what they see, hear, and their opinion of each candidate. Some are taken with a grain of salt and others have more influence than you would ever imagine. Make sure you greet them professionally and maintain a very friendly and professional attitude with EVERYONE you meet. You just never know when you may be speaking to the "top dog's" nephew or other close person within the organization. Everyone should be treated with the upmost respect and kindness.

As you are called back and enter the interview room, again greeting with a smile and handshakes. Pay close attention to who is in that room. Generally, you can expect multiple interviewers so pay attention to their names and actions. If you have done your homework pre-interview you will most likely have a good idea who they will be. If someone is there you didn't expect, pay attention to the name so you can thank them BY NAME upon exit.

In the actual interview follow the lead set by the hiring manager. They will give direction and most will provide some welcome conversation to help the candidate relax a little. This is done with the intent to get a feel for the personality of the candidate as much as helping them relax. Open up and be yourself at this point but never get unprofessional or lose your focus on what you came to do.

I have seen candidates get too relaxed and treat the interview too casual, to the point of disrespecting the process. Smiles and warm greetings are appropriate but it certainly needs to remain professional and focused on presenting your leadership and attributes that pertain to the position. On the flip side of the coin, I have seen many candidates so uptight and rigid that it made the interview uncomfortable and they struggle to impress as a result. Walk the fine line but allow your personality to show while maintaining a professional approach.

As the interview questions begin, remember to LISTEN to the question. Too often, candidates allow their minds to drift in the interview. What do I mean by drift? When asked a question and you provide your response, it's human nature to continue thinking about your response and what you may have left out or said wrong while the interviewers have moved on to the next question. Listen intently to each question, respond, then let it go! Although asking to have a question repeated is considered acceptable, having to ask several times during the interview because you are not staying on point is considered FAILURE.

How you respond to questions is another key ingredient often overlooked or not considered ahead of time. All candidates want to tell the interviewer "what they want to hear", but few candidates can say it correctly. Allow me to explain by sharing another example:

I was asked to participate in an interview a year or so ago that illustrates this point. We were interviewing for a manager position that would be responsible for leading a team of about twenty five employees and an operation serving thousands of customers generating millions in revenue. This position was critical to the success of the organization. Two candidates were very close in the running for the position and either could win the promotion with a good interview. The same question was asked of both candidates. I don't recall the exact wording but something like:

"Give us an example of a time you had to deal with conflict and what approach was taken to best resolve it."

Candidate #1 Response – *"If I was in a situation with a conflict occurring between two employees I would isolate the situation by separating the employees, remove them from the situation, meet with them individually, then bring them back together to resolve the difference so they could rebuild the relationship and work together moving forward".*

Candidate #2 Response – *"I would like to share a real life example of when I was placed in this situation. I saw two employees having a conflict and I approached the situation professionally. I took steps to isolate the situation by separating them, took them away from the other workers, met with them individually to figure out the problem, then brought them back together to resolve the issue and rebuild their relationship. In the individual conversations I realized it was a simple miscommunication and was easily resolved when we sat down together. Both employees apologized and shook hands, committing to each other and me that they would be less quick to react in the future before they got all the facts. It was a great experience and I know I handled it the right way with the desired outcome being accomplished. By the way, those two employees work very well together to this day and have had no further conflicts."*

Which candidate gets the promotion? Both responses are similar with nearly the exact same reaction to the conflict so why does Candidate #2 separate himself and get the promotion? It's "experiential knowledge" that makes the difference. Nothing paints a picture of a candidate like real life experiences shared. As mentioned previously, and why this is so important to gain "experiential knowledge" as you prepare for your next promotional opportunity. The very last statement made by the second candidate, *"By the way, those two employees work very well together to this day and have had no further conflicts."* That last statement speaks volumes AND paints the picture I'm looking for.

Now, don't get me wrong. If you haven't had an experience related to a question asked, you simply respond as Candidate #1 did by sharing what you would do in that situation. It is the best you can do honestly. However, I have seen candidates that I know personally have HAD experiences related to questions simply answer what they "would do". It's a costly mistake.

The key to providing good experiences that relate to the questions is good preparation in the mock interviews. You don't have time in the middle of the interview to consider all your past experiences. Good preparation and mock interviews will include writing down many of your leadership experiences from your life. Re-telling those stories to those helping you prepare will make them easily remembered when it counts.

If a candidate has to answer "what they would do" rather than "what they have done" to nearly every question I ask, they are simply not prepared for the promotion.

Upon completion of the interview questions, most interviewers will ask you if you have any final thoughts or questions for them. This becomes one last chance to separate yourself from the field.

First, ensure you thank each individual in the room personally by name for the opportunity and their time. Understand your closing comments are critical to leaving that lasting impression and instilling confidence in the hiring decision maker's mind. Express you enjoyed the process and could continue to discuss your qualifications all day if time permitted. This simple statement leaves them thinking you have much more to share and to offer that just simply was not asked or was unable to express in the time given. *"There's more in the tank",* as I like to say. Feel free to ask a couple questions but nothing too lengthy or personal. Show respect for the process and the people involved by keeping it simple, then close with what I call the **"character statement".**

The character statement is something that illustrates your character vs your job knowledge or experience. You have just spent the majority of the interview discussing your qualifications and experience. What really matters to most hiring managers or decision makers is your CHARACTER. I have heard my brother often say, *"I can teach a monkey to run the business but, I can't give him integrity and character."* What a true statement. I have awarded many promotions to a less experienced candidate who I had a good feeling about their character, loyalty, and passion vs the highly tenured veteran who may have me concerned about his character or attitude.

So how exactly do you close the interview with leaving that coveted "character statement"? Paint the picture with a short story. We are all suckers for a good "short" story that is interesting while relevant. Keep it short and keep it relevant and it will accomplish the goal. I'm going to share one of my favorites with you right now as an example:

A strong character statement closing to any interview:

"I'd like to take a couple minutes to share a quick story that really paints the picture for you as it relates to who I am and what I bring to your team. I once heard a story about how they train Arabian race horses. They start with a large group of horses and begin by teaching them basic commands, come to the trainer when the whistle blows, etc. Each day they train the horses physically by running them and working them to the point of exhaustion. Each training session is completed by allowing the horses to run to a large tub of water to refresh themselves and enjoy the break. After a few months of this systematic training regimen, one day they choose to alter the training. They will end the training by placing the horses in a tight coral with loose dirt and dust covering the ground. They then place the large tub of water up wind from the horses so they begin to smell the water and anticipate getting to drink! As you can imagine, these horses begin to get excited and start prancing around the coral. This movement in the tight space results in dust and dirt being kicked up in their noses causing their thirst to get more intense than ever! Just when the horses are about to break down the coral to get to the water, the trainer will release them. They take off! With all the horses now in a sprint to the water, the trainer will wait until they are just about to arrive then blow the whistle. Some of the horses will go a few more feet to get a few sips of water then come running to the trainer. Others will go to the water and fill their bellies before returning. Very few will stop dead in their tracks when they hear that whistle and although just a few feet from the water they so desperately desire, they will turn and return to the trainer without a single sip of water. Those few horses are the only horses that remain in the training and continue to become the coveted Arabian Race Horse! I tell

you that story because I want you to know that is the same level of dedication and commitment you will get from me from the very first day I begin working in your organization to the very last. It's who I am and who I will always be. I again thank you for this opportunity and hope you will allow me to join the ranks of your Arabian Race Horses!"

Now, how did that story make you "feel" as you read it? So often the candidates who get promoted are promoted off a "feeling" from those making the decision. Sharing personal experiences throughout the interview that "prove" you are in fact that type of "horse" will add additional value to this closing character statement. Again, tapping into that experiential knowledge and what you "have done" versus what you "will do".

When you face the facts, many have the basic qualifications for the positions, just as many horses can run fast. You separate yourself by adding the feeling to the mix. The character statement must bring the feeling to close the interview.

POST INTERVIEW

You have closed the formal interview and now waiting on the call to offer you the position. There are a few post interview steps to ensure you take, regardless of the outcome.

First, send "thank you" communications to the hiring manager or decision makers for the opportunity to interview and their time considering you for the promotion. Showing appreciation immediately after the meeting will leave one more positive interaction for those making the decisions. Will it change the outcome of their decision? Probably not. But it's clearly a good gesture and shows character. Promoting one's self is not about the "job" or "position". Following the outline and steps I have described WILL PROMOTE your life regardless of the change in title, and that's the real key to your progression.

A short time ago I had the opportunity to interview several candidates for a leadership position. Post-interview I was contacted by one of the candidates I had rejected for that position. He was following the proper steps for post-interview interaction by thanking me for the opportunity and requesting any feedback or coaching I could provide. I was impressed at his determination to find a victory in his defeat. In fact, I was so impressed I offered to meet him for lunch since he lived within driving distance. While having lunch and small talk I discovered he had been turned down for several similar management positions previously, each time being told he was just behind the winning candidates.

I began questioning his post-interview process for the previous opportunities. He informed me this was the first time he had taken the steps to follow up and try to "figure out" what he was "doing wrong". Amazing! The sad truth is that this example is more of the norm than the exception. How many continue to fail or simply drop out of the pursuit after a few rejections? The determination to never quit led this candidate to getting outside his comfort zone and seek the necessary coaching and feedback. This example also illustrates the second post-interview step I have yet to mention, the request for feedback and coaching. Most candidates simply take the rejection and move on, never considering the victory being left behind. The victory as described in the example is the FEEDBACK and COACHING.

Will every interviewer provide you with proper feedback and coaching? Absolutely not. However, there is no loss in asking. You will grow your network and learn valuable lessons from this potential interaction.

Does it pay off to follow these steps? Not only did he get a lunch meeting out of me, but multiple follow up visits and conversations and coaching. He was promoted officially into the very next management position he interviewed for a couple months later, changing his life forever. It works! He got outside his comfort zone, gained a mentor, grew his network, and won the next promotion.

The third essential step post-interview is proper communication after the promotion decision has been made. If you are not the successful candidate, contact the winning candidate to congratulate them. Most promotions from within organizations are fairly simple to find the winning candidate and send them a congratulatory email or phone call if you know them personally. Again, this simple interaction shows character, builds relationships, and promotes your life. If you follow the process outlined, YOU will most likely be the successful candidate! Therefore, it will be your responsibility to remain humble and work directly with the hiring manager by following their direction. Many times you will be asked to remain silent about the promotion until others are notified and other related steps are taken to announce the promotion. Begin building the relationship by building trust from day one.

In the event you are not the successful candidate, find your victory in the relationships you build throughout the process. In nearly every opportunity to promote in my life I have found a new friend or connection to add to my network while going through the process. Many of which have become very beneficial to my career and development, making every opportunity a victory at promoting my life.

ACCEPTING PROMOTION

I want to take a minute at this point to emphasize the importance of proper acceptance of promotion in your life and career. Let me take you back to the very beginning of this book when within the introduction I explained the three "regrets" in most people's lives.

-        I wish I had spent more time with the people I love.

-        I wish I had allowed myself to be happy.

-        I wish I had done more to reach my full potential.

Every promotion in life should "chip away" at these regrets. If not, the promotion is NOT a promotion, not the kind of promotion we are interested in. Accepting promotion is mental and physical. Accept who you are becoming and what roles and responsibilities come with each step along the way. The real key at this point is in **REMEMBERING** who you are and **WHY** promoting is important.

I once heard a parable about a merchant man who was seeking precious jewels. At last he had found the perfect pearl. He had the finest craftsman carve the most beautiful jewel box to display his pearl. He placed the pearl inside the box and began showing all who would come see his beautiful pearl. As time passed he noticed most people were complimenting the box more than the pearl. In fact, most ignored the pearl altogether and spent the time admiring the box. This response led the merchant to also focus more on the box than the pearl inside. The merchant found himself bragging on the box and shifting his time and attention from the pearl to the box. One day the merchant woke to an empty box. The pearl was gone! He suddenly felt lost and heartbroken from the loss of his most precious jewel. He had spent his life in search of precious jewels yet had become careless with the most precious jewel of all and lost it. He found himself lonely with an empty box and nothing left but regret and sorrow. The box suddenly was meaningless as he was quickly reminded of what was really important.

In promoting our lives, are we much like this merchant? Do we often lose sight of the "pearls" (family) in our lives while we shift our focus to the "boxes" (homes, cars, boats, career, etc.)? Many life promotions will provide you with the beautiful box that will get much more attention from others, while we lose focus on our pearls. Enjoy the boxes but **NEVER FORGET THE PEARLS!!**

I recall the early years of my marriage. My wife and I were dirt poor. We lived in a block apartment about the size of our current closet. You could hear the neighbors snore at night and we literally couldn't afford gas money to drive across town to visit my parents if it was the last week of the month. Conditions of our "box" were not desirable in any way! However, I had found my "pearl". The most precious jewel of my life and we were happy, as happy together then as we are now. The years of promotion have been good to us in many ways and our boxes are now a bit nicer and get more attention from others than those early boxes. However, for us, the boxes could be taken tomorrow and we would still remain just as happy knowing our pearls are in place. The pearl without the box is still a great life. The box without the pearl would be a disaster and complete failure. Never allow others to shift your focus from the pearls to the boxes!

KEYS TO BECOMING

*"If the thing you wish to do is right, and you believe in it, go ahead and do it. Put your dream across, and never mind what **they** say if you meet with temporary defeat, for **they**, perhaps, do not know that **EVERY FAILURE BRINGS WITH IT THE SEED OF AN EQUIVALENT SUCCESS!"** Unknown*

I often tell groups and individuals I don't care who you **ARE** rather my interest is in who you **ARE BECOMING.** At this point in our discussion of "promoting our lives" I want to step back long enough to really consider the roots and foundation needed to create lasting growth and progression. The only way to improve your life experience is to improve your life choices and change who you are **BECOMING**.

At times I witness individuals holding positions of rank or elevated status in the community or business that simply do not match the character of the person. Nothing is more disturbing and destructive to the people they influence, whether related to business, family, or community. How do they get those positions? Although their influence may be solely relying on the title rather than the true leadership, the question remains.

We all know charismatic individuals who can "put on" a front to get promoted, hired, elected, married, and more. The core of those individuals will always show up sooner or later. **NEVER** "fake it until you make it"! You are doing yourself and others a major injustice. Your character must be solid and **YOU** must work on your growth without pretending you're something you are not. Here are four keys, if followed, will guarantee your personal growth and who you are "becoming" will surely outpace your position of influence.

1. Commit to Work at Self-Development

In life there's nothing more permanent than change itself. What seemed impossible yesterday is the norm tomorrow. Jim Rohn said, *"A formal education can help you earn a living but self-education can help you earn a fortune."* Self-development is direct and dialed in to your area of interest, therefore the progression is much faster and the results immediate. Never stop learning, growing, asking questions, and being curious about the world around you. Many times in conversation I hear someone say "I know, I know." The point they are missing, it's not good enough to "know" in life! To "do" is the only way to create success and reach your potential. Congratulations! The fact you are reading this proves you are committed to this step.

The Chinese philosopher, Sun Tzu, once said, *"I hear and I forget, I see and I remember, but I do and I know".*

2. Go the Extra Mile

Most people will say they go the extra mile. Truth is, most actually don't even come close. And most people who do go the extra mile think, "Wait, no one else is here....why am I doing this?" and leave, never to return!

That is why the extra mile is such a lonely place. That is also why the "extra mile" is a place filled with opportunities. Be early, stay late. Make the extra call, send the extra email, do the extra research, and spend the extra time with those you love. Don't wait to be asked; offer. Don't just tell employees what to do, show them what to do and work beside them. Every time you do something, think of one extra thing you can do….especially if other people are **NOT** doing that thing. It's not easy, but it will pay off big time and make you incredibly successful.

"Successful people do what unsuccessful people are not willing to do. Don't wish it were easier, wish you were better". Jim Rohn

3. LIVE EVERY DAY WITH CHARACTER

I once read a story about a minister who became frustrated looking for a parking spot, and finally parked in a "no parking" zone. He left a note on his windshield which read: *"I'm a minister of the Gospel. Having circled the block five times and running late for a meeting, I had to park in this no-parking area. Forgive us our trespasses."*

On returning from his meeting three hours later, he noticed that a paragraph had been added to his note. It read: *"I'm a traffic officer and I've been policing this block for the past five years. If I don't give you a parking ticket I'll be dismissed from my job. Lead us not into temptation."*

You get the point, be honest in the small things as well as the big things. Living with integrity is often tested with the small things like admitting mistakes, living with honor when no one is looking, or standing for something when it's not popular.

4. SHED THE DEAD SKIN

I often use this example when I first meet new leaders or people I'm committing to mentor. Growing up I always wanted to have a pet snake. What young boy doesn't right! Of course, my mother was against the idea and clearly would never allow it. Once I moved out of the house and got my own place I made the purchase and finally had my snake. I didn't know much about snakes at the time but began noticing some things as it grew. I would feed it mice and eventually small rats about once a week as directed by the pet shop. I noticed about once a month its eyes would get hazy and the body would begin to look dull versus its normal shiny and vibrant appearance. This meant it was preparing to "shed the dead skin" and grow even bigger and more vibrant than before. Then one day it would decide the time was right and begin the shedding process. It always started with rubbing its head against a rock or hard surface to create the initial break in the skin. Once the initial break in skin was made on the head, the snake can basically slide right out of the dead skin and reach its new size and vibrant color.

The same can be said for all of us in our growth and progression. Individually, we all have "dead skin" holding us back from our growth and becoming more vibrant. To reach our potential we must identify our dead skin and remove it. For individuals it can be attitude, pride, bad habits, negative influences, and much more. Teams also have "dead skin" that must be removed to progress. I explain to management teams that they are the head of the snake. The shedding starts with them using their minds and available tools to identify the skin that needs to be removed, then taking the action! For organizations or teams it can be poor processes, poor products, poor performers, organizational attitude, and much more. For both individuals and organizations the shedding of the dead skin **must start at the head**, must be a recurring process, and must include everything keeping them from growing and reaching their potential.

5.   BE DETERMINED

A life worth living is not easy! If you find your life is easy, you simply are not challenging yourself or reaching your full potential. In order to experience success and promote your life it will take hard work and a lot of **DETERMINATION**. Determination is tied directly to **RESOLVE**. Many years ago I had someone place a pencil on a desk and ask me to "try" to pick it up. Not knowing where this conversation was going, I simply reached over and picked it up. *"No! I said try to pick it up"*, was the response. I replied, *"I did pick it up"* a bit confused. I was asked to put it back on the desk and "try" to pick it up again. After a few attempts, it was explained to me there is **NO TRY**. Either you do it or you don't do it. You either pick it up or you don't pick it up. We live in a world of **TRY** while the real winners walk a path of **RESOLVE**.

That simple lesson has stuck with me for many years and I use it to this day when someone tells me they will "try" to do something. The type of resolve needed to truly reach your potential in life is the same type of resolve Henry Ford had regarding the V8 motor and the same resolve "Billy" had in the short stories previously shared.

I have spent many years working with and around top performers and very accomplished and successful people. Every one of those individuals who become the highest achievers with the highest levels of success are those who do things that the low achievers simply don't want to do. They walk the roads less traveled. They all live each day with purpose and never give up in pursuit of their goals. Many get knocked down and hit road blocks but it's never a question of whether they will bounce back but rather HOW HIGH they will bounce back.

I recently noticed a sign on the wall of my son's Tae Kwon Do gym that perfectly illustrates this point. It reads, *"A Black Belt is a White Belt that never gave up!"* Head Master Kim and his team are great mentors and trainers for my son. His gym, Moohan Martial Arts Academy, trains students to have no limits and progression without end. Determination is the key to endless progression for us all.

Ever heard of the infomercial company Beachbody? This is the company that created and sold P90X. Little known fact, they FAILED over twenty times at marketing P90X before it took off. The number of failures is debated with some reporting it failed over 100 times! I read an article from one of the founders Carl Daikeler stating it was over twenty, so I will stick with that number for this example. To date, P90X has generated over $700 MILLION in sales!

Now consider your goals and visions. If you failed twice, three times, seven times, or maybe fifteen times, would you continue pursuing that goal? Why do so many start-up businesses fail in the first couple years? *"Low achievers will not do what high achievers are willing to do"*. The majority of businesses do not even turn a profit until the third or fourth year, while over fifty percent close shop in the first two years. Step back and think about the statistics, its mind blowing.

With that said, review your vision and goals of promoting your life and test your determination. Ask yourself how many failures would it take for you to give up on your dream? **What's YOUR NUMBER?** Imagine the difference in so many million people's lives had Carl given up on P90X after the twentieth failure! Not to mention the loss of $700 Million in sales for his company! I'm certainly glad he remained determined since I'm a thankful customer of his business and products.

I share these examples and stories at this point because it's critical to your success that you understand challenges occur when you begin the process of change. Many of your challenges will come from those you think will be most supportive. When you begin to promote your life and change who you are becoming, you will be met with adversity and doubt. Although I have been blessed with very supportive friends and family over the years, I have seen many others face the direct opposite. Sadly, many close to you now are not going to be happy when your life choices begin to change and those choices create distance from their choices. This is where **MOST FAIL** and fall back into life with the sheep!

My advice on this subject is simple. Include those you love in your vision and challenge them to join you. Grow and promote together. Compare these changes to someone who wants to stop smoking. If that person has two friends that they take smoke breaks with each day, it would be important to discuss the reasons they are going to quit and ask their friends to join them in the mission. The success rates sky-rocket when you have the support and commitment from those closest to you. Refer back to the silent committing discussion for more pointers on staying the course.

Bottom line, you may have to distance yourself from many who are influences in your life currently. If you are not prepared for that action, you are not prepared for real change or promotion.

"Keep away from people who try to belittle your ambition. Small people always do that, but really great people make you feel that you, too, can become great." Mark Twain

CONCLUSION

1. Have Fun!

I have found the most success and most happiness in my life when I was having fun! Don't disregard this as overly simple or even childish. As I stated earlier, promoting your life is an art not science. Creating a fun atmosphere proves to elevate the morale and produce improved results. I was watching a championship fight the other night and in between rounds listening to the coach of the champ direct him to "relax and have fun". He continued by saying, "When you fight relaxed and just have fun in there, no one can beat you". A truth in sport and in life!

2. Treat Your Time Like Your Bank Account!

Time is our greatest asset, period. How you choose to use your time will ultimately determine the speed and success of your life's promotion. Take a minute to calculate what you believe your time is worth per hour. Let's just say on a low scale everyone's hour is worth at least $50. With that said, if every hour you spent watching television or "surfing" the net literally withdrew $50 from your bank account, how much time would you spend doing those things? If every hour you slept past the needed seven to eight hours cost you $50 from your account, how late would you sleep on Saturday / Sunday morning? Of course there are countless examples I could use for "wasting time" so I leave it to you to complete your own inventory of the hours you spend. If they are not adding value and drawing you nearer to your ultimate potential and life's vision, just don't do it!

"Until you value yourself, you won't value your time. Until you value your time, you will not do anything productive with it". M. Scott Peck

3. Be Humble!

You can choose to be humble or you can choose to be humbled. Keeping yourself humble is really just being honest if you think about it. I remember the first couple times I met a "star" or famous person. Two things became very apparent to me in those situations. First, I realized they are not that special once they are off the T.V. screen and in front of me like anyone else. Second, those I met that were humble and much more "down to earth" were much more impressive to me. When we remain humble, we gain further understanding and wisdom. Our network continues to grow and our life promotion is endless. The quickest way to failure is through isolation. The quickest way to isolation is arrogance and pride. My best tool for remaining humble has always been a good memory. Never forget the journey or the people that brought you to your state of promotion.

4. Believe in Yourself and Others!

Developing confidence and real belief in self is one of the most empowering steps you will ever take. It's a step that must be taken over and over again as you progress and promote your life, so master it and go to it for support when there's no one else standing with you. I began this work describing the art of "changing your mind" and will close it similarly. Developing a personal truth about your self will drive your actions and results. Never sell yourself short in this regard. I believe we are all divine children of the Almighty God with infinite potential. That means NOTHING is impossible and every single one of us have divine DNA with infinite potential.

"We all have a personal truth. A truth that we believe about ourselves. We generate the results in life that we believe we deserve." Dr. Phil McGraw

5. There is NO END and NO LIMITS!

When it comes to progression and promotion, there is no end, no retirement, and no conclusion! It will only end when YOU say it does. In 1953 journalists of the time were convinced the four-minute mile was the limit to human speed. In 1954 Roger Bannister broke down that wall and ran the mile in under four minutes simply by not believing the hype of the journalist or the myth that humans had a limit. The very following year a few DOZEN athletes followed his lead and broke the four-minute mile. These examples are endless, and always track back to individuals who eliminated all limits placed on them by others. When you think you have reached the highest level, think again. There is always another level.

Dr. David Keirsey describes sixteen personality traits in his work *The Sixteen Types.* In his description of the *Promoter,* he describes this trait similarly with the art of influence in which I've explained.

Promoters are easily the most persuasive, the most winning, able to put forward an enterprise, and then to win others' confidence to go along with what they propose. In a sense, Promoters are able to operate people with much the same skill as Crafters operate machines, vehicles, weapons, and other tools. It might be said that people are instruments in the hands of Promoters, and that they play them artistically.

The greatest leaders in history all understood leading self and others is about influence and the *art* of promoting. They understand the responsibility that comes with promoting and influence and always lead for the right reasons. I pray we all take the tools we've been given and techniques outlined in this work to "lead the people" and **PROMOTE OUR LIVES.**

ABOUT THE AUTHOR

Rather than list all his accolades such as College Degrees, Professional Certifications, countless leadership awards from over 17 years of experience in leadership positions and roles, and many other personal and professional accomplishments....

BRANDON TOLBERT's desire is that this section be about what is truly important in his life. What he wishes to pass to his family as a legacy. His being:

- **A loyal husband**
- **A dedicated father**
- **An honorable son**
- **A great friend**
- **A devout Christian**
- **A committed mentor**

www.ingramcontent.com/pod-product-compliance
Lightning Source LLC
Chambersburg PA
CBHW051730170526
45167CB00002B/873